Slipping Thru The Veil

Awaken to the Spiritual World Beyond

Dane Whitecloud

Editor, Andrea Susan Glass, www.WritersWay.com

BALBOA
PRESS
A DIVISION OF HAY HOUSE

Balboa Press books may be ordered through booksellers or by contacting:

Balboa Press
A Division of Hay House
1663 Liberty Drive
Bloomington, IN 47403
www.balboapress.com
1 (877) 407-4847

Because of the dynamic nature of the Internet, any web addresses or
links contained in this book may have changed since publication and
may no longer be valid. The views expressed in this work are solely those
of the author and do not necessarily reflect the views of the publisher,
and the publisher hereby disclaims any responsibility for them.

The author of this book does not dispense medical advice or prescribe the use
of any technique as a form of treatment for physical, emotional, or medical
problems without the advice of a physician, either directly or indirectly. The
intent of the author is only to offer information of a general nature to help you
in your quest for emotional and spiritual well-being. In the event you use any
of the information in this book for yourself, which is your constitutional right,
the author and the publisher assume no responsibility for your actions.

Any people depicted in stock imagery provided by Thinkstock are models,
and such images are being used for illustrative purposes only.
Certain stock imagery © Thinkstock.

Print information available on the last page.

ISBN: 978-1-5043-3146-3 (sc)
ISBN: 978-1-5043-3147-0 (e)

Library of Congress Control Number: 2015905909

Balboa Press rev. date: 6/23/2015

Contents

Section II: Spiritual Learning Rituals

Section III: Personal Experiences

Prologue

My view and perception of life

This is my journal of Dreams, Visions and Thoughts. I started writing ideas down in the early 1990s. It's so easy to forget memories years later. These are, of course, all my points of view. To me, everything recorded here is all real. My goal is telling you how it was with no sugar coating or trying to make it fit other people or their feelings. Some of it is very disturbing, while other passages are uplifting or inspiring. How you look at the world is a personal thing. These experiences were very personal to me. I have cried, I have laughed and I have thoroughly enjoyed all these moments.

If you're reading this, accept my love for you and keep an open mind. I truthfully thank you. We are all one, yet we are individuals. May you enjoy life, hope and happiness, and find true love within yourself. I do it with each moment of my existence.

This journal of experience is done in 3 sections and does not have to be read cover to cover. Each part or chapter can be read by itself, being led by your spirit within yourself to feel or understand. The 1st part is a few of the 1,000's of dreams or visions I have had over the years of my life. The 2nd part is the learning rituals or gifts of energy movement and how to use or do them, hands on workshop of learning. The 3rd part is my personal thoughts, feelings and what caused my changes within, becoming awakened with all the good and bad of a total change of life.

I am, I am a man, I am a soul learning
and exploring who I am within.
Dane Whitecloud
We all are one.

My Mantra

"To know God is to know self"

"To know self is to know God"

"To see is to see"

"To hear is to hear"

"To feel is to feel"

"Insight remains"

"Insight moves to understanding"

"Understanding leads to compassion"

"Compassion is caring"

"Caring expands life creations"

"Life is God"

"Life is self"

"God-self is life"

"Creatively"

"We are one"

"May, creative life, expand within the one"

Dane Whitecloud

Section 1

My Dreams, Visions and Thoughts

The Journey Begins

It is quiet. I am ready to travel, to visit and see friends, those beyond this physical world. My eyes are closed, yet open to anticipating today's new journey. At first, I am having trouble calming down from my day, thinking about what was going on, you know, day-to-day stuff. My life is like most people: working, eating and experiencing the challenges of seeing new and old friends. Letting go of these activities is hard to do worrying about why this happened and why life is like this. Yet knowing I am the only one who makes my day, good, bad or troublesome. I am just going over my thoughts and thinking as I sit down, then roll into bed.

I am calm and at peace as I understand the easy flow of life. Once having that feeling, I am ready, ready to explore the realms of light and sound. Having been on many trips over the years, they are like visions that play through me, seeing many different places and times. They are clear images of the past, present and future. Some are with my body and some are not. It all depends on where I am and who I am with. Let the visions begin.

Visions and dreams can happen anytime for me. They average three to six every day now. At first, they only happened once a month. You may wonder how this all got started. My belief is that everyone is traveling, not just me. The real difference is: I remember. Most people choose not to, or they do not know how. Over time, I have found that the mornings are best for me, 6:00 a.m. until about 12:00 noon. Just as I get to bed, I ponder a wake-up time. Let us say 6:00 a.m. When that time comes, my mind says get up and go to the restroom or get a drink of water, then go back to bed to rest. This sets the mood for me to travel. I am aware it is time to travel. I then set my mind to travel. It works for me.

The different ways I rest can be lying on my back, side or stomach. What seems to work for me is having my hands, or at least my fingertips, open and not closed in a fist. My arms are reaching down towards my feet. The bottoms of my feet are also free, not crossed over. This gives me a feeling of energy. It passes in through my body from one extremity and out the other.

This flow of energy, I think, helps me when traveling. It is as if my body goes to sleep but my mind is still very active. I am aware of lying down in bed or wherever I am. Yet, I can go anywhere.

You may wonder where I go. Anywhere I wish, though there are limits. I have learned over a period of time that there are windows and doors. Windows are places, times and things you can see but may not enter or interact with. Doors are places, times and things you can enter into and interact with. You do have to know when the door is open and not closed. Imagine yourself in a hallway with doors and windows on each side of the hallway. You drift through the hallway, seeing some open doors and closed ones and also seeing windows. You may stop as you are passing at any time, looking through the windows or stepping through an open door. This is how the travel process works. You may ask if it is the same hallway each time. No, it changes. Some hallways you can enter for just a few seconds, others can be open for years. That is why it is hard to get back to a vision or a dream. You lose the hallway. You may be in a totally different hallway or a new one you have never been in before. Your thoughts might want to get back to the last one, but you cannot. It is better to relax, find calmness and start a new one or end the journey.

So, I am ready, relaxed and calm within, and the energy is flowing through me. My eyes are closed. Starting to see little lights, focusing on the lights and the feeling of being weightless. The more I have this feeling, the more I start to move. The more I move, the more lights I see. This goes on for a little while. I focus on the lights and movement. Back and forth until they blend together. The journey has started.

Now, I mentioned a hallway with windows and doors. These are within each of us. Within moments of the journey, your path is there for you. You do not need to think of this hallway with doors and windows. It is already there. So, engage the feeling, follow the light and see where it takes you.

Let me give you some examples of the places, people and times of some of my journeys.

The Mansion Worlds

I float down a hallway, seeing an open door and enter. I am in a Realm of Light, a place of space and what many would call a Mansion World. You may think of it like heaven. I am in front of a home of rest for someone. I'm walking through a beautiful yard and landscape and next to me is my son Jonathan. We reach out and hold hands. My son is six years old.

In this vision, we looked at each other and smiled. We went to the front door near a porch area. At the end of the porch way was a man working with his garden. He looked up and saw us, stopped what he was doing and walked over to us. It was my father. At first he was a little surprised to see us. In moments though, he seemed okay with our being there. All of us embraced and shook hands. You see my dad had passed on in the mid-1980s. Jonathan never really knew him, he had passed to this world years before his birth. This place was my father's home in the mansion worlds. He wanted to know how we were, so we talked. Jonathan on earth does not really talk or speak very well as he is autistic, but here, he did talk. We all talked and enjoyed each other's company.

After our talk, Jonathan and I decided to go for a walk together. We talked and talked. We told each other we would visit together again and said good-bye. Walking a little further and the light began to get brighter. Movement, feeling weightless and then back at home in my bed again. This journey was over. I got up to get a drink of water and thought of what just happened. The feeling was wonderful. You see, I had not seen Jonathan in months. I am a divorced man who could only see his kids when my work schedule did not fall on weekends. And it had been at least six months since I had seen my father. It was nice.

You may wonder: "Where were you? You were brought with your son to visit your father who had died?" Yes, you can travel to realms of light and darkness. You can visit or see in the heavens and beyond. You can visit any time the doors are open in your hallway. You can visit any time, place or person, living or dead in the eyes of the world. The real question is: "Is your father dead or a ghost?" The answer is "no", he is a spiritual being. We were just visiting where he lives now. He is a spiritual being and he lives. When my father passed away out of this life, he was transported to another place. A place that is very special. In the realms of light and sound to what most people call "Heaven". I just like to call them the Mansion Worlds. They are full of life. Everyone who has ever lived on this planet has had the opportunity to go to these worlds.

You can visit them anytime, while still alive. Many of you already have and do not even realize it. Most of us have been to these realms, thousands and thousands of times. I will try to describe them to you later.

Let us go, within ourselves, and find the hallways, windows and doors. See, hear, feel and understand that life is eternal.

A Place of Silence

Here is more about my travels of which there are so many. As I said before there are thousands upon thousands of places to go. Let us start with a new and different place. Moving with the feeling, the light is here. The hallway and door open. I enter.

The light is going by me at great speed. The light is beautiful. It is streaming and floating by me, slowing down, and then stopping in front of a very large cave. This place is not like any place I have ever seen before. The first thing I notice is it is really quiet. It has a special tone, just a very soft light tone with no pattern, yet it feels great. Two images or beings come over near me. They are not like me. I feel or sense them and their presence. They do not look like people or like any being with a body. They are like pure light, and nothing like anyone I have encountered before. They motion for me to enter the cave.

I'm feeling really good and push myself off the ground below my feet. Seeming to be floating in the air toward the cave opening, I look down and see that the cave has water flowing into it. It looks like water, but maybe it is not. There are no paths to walk on; you have to float in. It is such a wonderful feeling. The smell of pure energy passes over and through my body. It is touching the very pores of my body and cells. I am still floating and looking down all around me seeing small lights. They are like little fire candles spotted everywhere. They are on the walls and on the energy water below. What a fantastic sight, passing through one big cave into another, floating in and out. There are many different levels. Each one has its own light, smell and feeling. Time passes after traveling into maybe 100 or more caves. Slowing down, finding a spot to sit, I observe the two beings floating over to me. They sit on each side of me, looking at me and observe my feelings.

There is no talking here in this realm. Not one word is spoken or to me. Yet, I know where I am and who is with me. This information is just given to me and I understand. A long time passes, yet it seems like no time, as I rise up and look at my friends, glowing. I start floating back to the other end of the caves and go out. The light is rushing by me again and soon I am home.

I must tell you that this was a wonderful experience for me. You see, this was a place of silence and pure energy. It is a moment of stillness in a place where all energy passes through. It was a gift to me, an initiation to the beings of energy and of my feeling like I was one of them.

You may ask: "Where is this place?" I am not sure, but we are all connected to it. It does seem so very far away. You may ask: "Who are those beings?" They are the caretakers of the flow of energy, light and sound. They do much more and are timeless. They control the flow of all existence. I have heard other people talk about them. Some have called them the Og Min. It is probably just one of their names. The name seems right to me. The pleasure of their company will always be in my heart, and I hope to visit them again sometime. I have found that there are so many different places, with different kinds of beings. It is so exciting to be part of this experience, and I hope that someday, you too, will see what I have seen. You will love it!

A Place of Transport

Let us change our thinking and open up to the idea. What truth is can change today. Let us look at a different point of view. It can be hard to do at first, so just let it unfold in front of you. Then ponder it latter. Go back in your mind and readjust your understanding. We do it all the time. This time do it with focus.

My travels have shown me that I am an explorer, going through the realms of light and always observing all possible views of my experience. So far I have written about one realm in the Mansion Worlds and one realm in a far off place.

Many of my travels have been as a guide for others into different realms and places. Let me describe one of those. There is a place of transport for those traveling to certain destinations. I love this spot and have brought many people there.

There is a place on this planet in the northern hemisphere that is a realm of light, and many different kinds of people go there. Some of the people have died, and their spirits are traveling to distant spots within space and time. Some come here to go to very specific realms of light and darkness. And there are many other reasons to be there. It is a very busy place. To get to their destinations, they must get into a special transport. It is how we can travel to some of the realms we can see and others we cannot. You go through a hallway, then a door, and you feel movement. Then you see the lights and hear a high pitched tone. It is so quick, you do not even perceive it. Then you are brought to this place of transport and most of the time you do not even realize where you are. It happens so fast, yet what happens in seconds can be slowed down. You can see it in slow, slow motion, as if time had slowed down to a crawl. There is a place where people are waiting or even watching others depart and leave. Picture an airport or maybe even a shuttle port in a little valley. You can see the little lights travel out toward their destinations, similar to a light show. One after another they go, and even some at the same time. What a wonderful sight and a must-see place to visit.

These travel transports are in fact living beings. They have the ability to travel beyond the speeds of light. You climb into the body of the creature and it cradles you safely. These are very special creature beings. I love how they feel, and how they fly is way beyond what anyone could think. It is truly a fun way to fly. It is not the only way to travel, but is one of the most common ones. If in your travels you wish to visit and watch the lights, you will not be disappointed. All you have to do to get there is slow down before you travel. Request that you want to see the transport station, and slow down to a slow motion kind of focus. Maybe I will see you there and be your guide too.

It is interesting that the transport beings seem to have wings as they move. Maybe that is why people think angels have wings when they go to heaven. As you sit cradled inside of them, you can see the person inside. The beings are translucent.

Sort of like water having form. This is hard to describe, but if you saw them you would know what I mean. They are truly beautiful creatures. So, that is one of the ways you can travel. I want to travel again and again. I am ready, are you?

A Deeper Look at the Mansion Worlds

Jesus is said to have spoken, "In my Father's house there are many Mansions." How true that statement is. So let me tell you a little more about the Mansion Worlds. There are many more than you might think. The worlds and the mansions are really diverse in size, population and levels of time and space.

Let us talk about levels first. There are no good or bad levels. Even in the lowest levels, they are not any better spiritually than the higher ones. The levels are set up by light and vibration. They are there to uplift and encourage the human spirit within each of us.

The worlds within the levels are like schools: first grade, second grade, third and so on. A first grader is not any better a spirit than the fourth grader. Their level of space and time experiences are different. There is a balance of caring and comfort within each individual. They just have different things to learn and experience. Age has no place here either. Each spirit's vibration is in them. The spirit body forms to the ideal age within each person. They could be a new born, or a 100 years old in the way they look.

Not only are people separated by experience vibrations, there are knowledge vibrations too. Many different factors help place you in a realm of light. There are religions there too, and you may have an experience that could give you a belief or behavior that may move you to a certain place. There are some religions that are together, while others are separate. Every one of them is there in some way. Time also separates them. Let us say, there are old Indian realms and new ones. People who passed on 100 years ago have different thoughts of what they believe in. What your beliefs is helps place you in these worlds and levels. For the most part, all of them are beautiful. There are other levels and realms are dark with very little light. Any of these places can be visited with the right desires to see them.

There are two ways to visit. One is as the guest "observer", the other is to be a part of the experience. As the guest observer you cannot interact with the beings in the realm. When you are part of the experience, you can talk and are one of beings and look like them in appearance. At first you will always be in the guest observer role. Once you are comfortable and you understand the process and how it works, you will be permitted to go to the next step and engage as a being who can be part of the experience by interacting.

There are hundreds and thousands of levels, realms and worlds. You can visit as many as you desire. It is up to you. What kind of experience do you want to have?

A few of the realms of interest are:

1. The children's worlds.
2. Temples or halls of art, science and history.
3. Religious places.

4. Music halls or gardens.
5. Hall of personal records.

All of these places are fun and exciting to see. You will be given a guide to help you have the best experience. This guide is one of the first gifts you receive on all visits. You may ask questions and to understand more about what you may be looking at observing. Most of your guides will have a name. I have had many different guides, all of whom are always giving of their time and energy. They want you to understand all you are seeing and doing on your visits. You will not have the same guide on all visits. I also have been a guide and it is fun and enjoyable to help someone.

So, put away your thought of what heaven might be someday. You can experience it now, not when you pass away. Now is the time for you to gain insight into yourself. Do it while you are here and now. Once you have started to see, hear and understand, the world you live in today will change. It is because you have changed inside. The journey has begun. You have become an explorer.

"Where are these mansion worlds?" you may ask. I asked the same question a number of years ago. They are very close to the planet earth. It fact, we live in a sort of mansion world. The world we live in today has a light and vibration to it. The vibration of this world is easy to find. Sit down and listen to your world around you. Listen for a buzzing, high pitched ringing tone. That is the sound vibration of the planet earth. You can even feel it if you take off your shoes and really focus.

Once you know what it sounds like and what it feels like, you will pick it up everywhere. Go outside, indoors or on a high mountain. It is all around you. Each realm or world has a vibration and sound of its own, like earth.

We are in a mansion world. You may ask: "Where are the other worlds?" There are five major continents on this planet and there is a mansion world over each of them. Asia, Europe, Africa, North America and South America each has one on top of them. They are very large at the bottom and get smaller at the top. They cover a large area of land and some of the water. Each level has thousands of realms, looking something like this:

***** Top

****

****

****

*********************** Bottom

Each Continent / Water

There are many of them to see and visit. Observe or interact with all of the five continents or just one. Seeing them for yourself is always the best experience: "A picture is worth a thousand words." But so is being there.

My Mother's Gift

I have only told a few people this story over the years. It happened around 1995. I was working at a Kits Camera store in Tyler Mall, in Riverside, California. I was 42 and living with a woman named Vicki in an apartment. Having been married for 14 years, my divorce papers were just finalized a month earlier. I had not lived with my ex-wife for almost four years. It was an emotional time for me, and my kids thought I'd let them down as their father. Not being there for them every day, I overcompensated with them when we did get together. I really loved them, and it was hard to drop them off every other week on visits. I took them everywhere they could have fun like the beach, the mountains and the great outdoors. The divorce was hard on all of us, and I spent many nights crying hoping that someday my kids would understand.

The night was warm, and I had just showered to get ready for bed. I was sitting on the end of my bed and pondering my day. A few minutes passed and I happened to look to my right side and saw my mother sitting next to me. She said, "Hello, it's good to see you." I replied the same. She said, "I've come to give you a gift." Looking at her I was surprised. "What gift?" I asked. This is what she told me. "What I give to you is only for you and no one else. You can't tell anyone you have this gift inside you. It's the gift of sight! You will be able to see the guides and angels that work with all the people around you. You will only have this gift for one day. It's yours today only and never again in this life." I looked at her and smiled. "Wake up in the morning and through your whole day you will see the spirits of light. All of them are working with every person you meet or talk with. You will see them all, and this will be for your understanding. You are not alone and your guide has requested this gift for you. When the day ends and you go back to sleep, the gift will leave you. Remember to tell no one while this gift is in you. It's for you to see the love, caring and help that's given in this world to every soul that lives." She smiled at me and said, "I love you." I said I loved her too, and with that she was gone. My mother was a wonderful woman, and she had passed out of my life years earlier in 1991. It was nice to see her again.

The next day was truly amazing and a wow moment for me. Waking up, I saw my girlfriend Vicki sleeping next to me. She had two light workers next to her. It was a beautiful sight. I got dressed and headed out to work living only a few short blocks away. It was early and not very many people were around. There were just a few people doing their daily walk in the mall. The guides and light beings were right next to them as they passed by. Some of them had only one guide with them, and others had up to 10 beings around them. Everyone I saw had someone with them. Even the children had someone helping them. As the day continued for me, it started to get harder to stay focused. The mall was getting full of people, with so many light workers and people all at the same time. I was feeling overwhelmed with the spirit of love and compassion.

My work was in the sale of cameras as well as photo printing at the camera store. My concentration was being tested. Looking at my guide, he was helping me stay focused. He would point out different people from time to time. He wanted me to see the interaction of the spirit and the person they were helping. Some of the guides were softly touching the person. Others were just ahead of them as they walked. Some light workers were even conversing and communicating to other light workers. It was a total interaction of people, light beings and guides.

As I was having lunch, I sat and watched it unfolding in front of me. It was truly beautiful, and I wished everyone in the world could see it for five minutes. I was almost in tears a few times. I did not tell anyone around me, though it was hard not to say anything. Then I went back to work, and at the end of the day went home. It was such a wonderful day for me. What a gift. I took my shower, then went to bed. Sleep came quickly, and it was over. The next day it was gone, and I never had the gift again.

I never told anyone at that time, however a few people would find out what had happened. It was years later that I allowed myself to talk about it, but only if the spirit within moved me to do so. That is why you are hearing about it now. People like me need to know we are not alone, and we need to tell others. Not even for a moment of your life are you alone.

Understand that with everything you do, there is a being of light with you. They do not judge you and want to help in any way possible and may whisper in your ears, touch you lightly or keep you from harm. Let you be who you are. These beings care about you and the experience you are having with life. I want to say, "Thank you, thank you so much for being there for me." My guide just touched my heart and smiled. We have a wonderful connection.

We Are Not Alone

My visions and dreams are so overwhelming to me. Wow! I can see the smallest particle in the universe like an electron circling an atom. Or I can be a part of something on a larger scale, like watching energy planets, galaxies or star systems many light years away. You can do this too which is a way to learn about yourself and how things work, to understand about the future, present or past.

On this planet, we have been growing and trying to reach out to the stars. People have grown so much in the last 100 years. Humans have invented airplanes, cars, rockets and satellites and we are even trying to communicate and listen to other solar systems in space. I need to say, "We are not alone". There are so many different living creatures out in the stars above.

We have been searching for what we call extraterrestrial intelligence, "S.E.T.I " for short. We are using radio waves to see if we can make contact or receive any messages from another world. This will be very difficult to do. Every planet has a unique vibration and evolution to life. There are many factors that determine life and how it grows. Gravity, water, sunlight and even how the energy field surrounds a cell can affect how life will be.

How life grows in other worlds is not like how it is in our world. The human experience on earth is unique. I am not saying there are not humanoid beings out there. There are many of them. Some are like us in a few ways. Many are not even close to what we are. We are trying to contact and communicate with beings that did not grow and learn like us. The S.E.T.I. program is a nice thought, but I'm not sure it will succeed at its goal of contact.

Let us look at ourselves. We have grown over the years from cave dweller to house builder and have learned to use our planet. We use its water, air and the earth itself to get a better life each day. Think of how our technology enables us to do things today that were unthinkable years ago. Yet when looking at human beings, they have not grown within as much. Where is our happiness and joy at living? Becoming wealthy in food, housing and traveling around the globe is not growth. That may be short term happiness or a quick fix. Yet, how you live your life and perceive it within is the truth of what it means to change and grow as human beings.

Every living thing has a vibration and happiness and joy within. As human beings we have not really learned to experience any long term deep feeling of love for ourselves and others. We have been taught that life is hard and we must learn to survive. Only through pain and suffering can we learn to be happy. This is not true! You do not have to have a bad experience to know a good one. There are no bad or good experiences. They are just living experiences. You can know happiness in any place, time or situation. You have the power within your being to experience happiness. Anytime it is there, and you do not have to depend on anyone else to give it to you.

Let us talk about making contact with beings from other planets. There are many different kinds of planets and solar systems. Some are similar to ours and many are not. How can we reach them with our technology? We could send a rocket and make contact, however that will take a long time to get close enough and to communicate. We could use our current way of communication by using short wave radio or some kind of laser. I believe there is a way as other planets already use those technologies. We may have already received messages and do not even know it. We just need to figure out how it is done and used. What is the common connection that unites the people of other worlds to us? It is our sun and the stars. You see the stars every night out in space. You see the sun and feel the warmth and ultraviolet rays each day. The stars and sun provide clean usable energy that moves very fast. This energy can be used to communicate.

We have learned how to use the resources of our planet, and now we need to learn how to use the sun and its energy. Communication with the stars is possible. We can send or receive messages through light. When we do this, we will make contact and this will be our link to each other. We can already see many stars and solar systems out in space, and they can see us. As human beings, we need to research sun communication. Our government may already have done this, yet the public may not even know it is being done.

Many people on this world think we have beings from

other worlds here now. Some have had direct contact or communication with them. I have yet to experience them on this planet. We think our technology is so wonderful now: we have cell phones, radio, TV, computers and electric energy. When we truly have control of the sun's energy, all of that will be used for the good of man. We will also learn how to travel to the stars. Light and vibration are the keys to open the door to other worlds and will change all that we know now. Are you ready to communicate? We are not alone, and the vastness of outer space is within our reach. Many planets do this now traveling within light and vibration.

You travel in your dreams and visions now, by light and vibration. You are using the light and vibration within you. I feel it within me every day and hope you feel it within you too.

Extraterrestrial Encounter

During all my travels in the realms and other worlds I have not run into what humans call ETs. Yet, I have talked with many people who said they have had experiences with them. A woman known as Evie Lorgen wrote books on abductions and encounters with aliens. I met her at the Philosophical Library in Escondido, California. She was giving a class on how to stay away from the tall Grays or the shorter ETs. She stated she had been abducted many times and knew what to look for when you saw something that was odd or different. I was speaking alone with her for many hours at a beautiful park with a lake one day, and she was surprised I had not run into any of them before. She remarked on how maybe they were not too interested in me or what I may have had to offer them. I am so spiritual; she said inside maybe they were probably looking for certain DNA found in certain human beings, maybe ones not so spiritually evolved.

My mind started to wonder if aliens existed, or if I might someday see one or have an encounter. A year or two went by, and then I started to think about extraterrestrials again. Going to my computer and getting online late one night, I checked my emails and there was one titled "Cosmic Waters". A different woman with the name Eve had sent the message. Thinking it was odd that she had the same name as the woman I met at the Philosophical Library, I looked closely at the message. She wrote that she was working with the tall gray beings that were from another dimension. Intrigued, I replied to the email telling her I was very spiritual yet I never encountered any of the beings she described. I said I would be open to meeting some of them. She responded that it might be possible. She helped them, and they approved of her working to find humans that would be open to helping them. In my next email, I asked "Eve, what do you help them to do"? She avoided my question and responded by saying that there was a place in space and time where she and I could visit with the Grays. Would I want to go and do a ritual with them? I said I would enjoy having the experience. We arranged a time and place to meet them in the San Diego area.

The room where we met was very small and had only one door and one window. It was about the size of an office, in fact, it looked a little like a hospital room. It had bright overhead lights and a desk in one corner. There were a few shelves above the desk, and to one side there were longer and deeper shelves that contained white towels. There was a black office chair near the desk where Eve sat. In the middle of the room there was a long wooden table that reminded me of a massage table. I sat facing her, and she said that this is the place we could meet the gray beings, and we needed to prepare to do the ritual. Telling me to grab a towel and undress, she then left the room. Once I was undressed, I sat on the edge of the table with the towel covering only my buttocks and part of my legs. She came back in a few minutes and asked me to lie face down and to put my face in the head support on the end of the table. From that position, I could only see the light around me. Eve said it was time to begin.

I was told it was necessary to listen to every word she said. As she asked each question, she told me to answer yes each time and to make sure she heard me. I do not remember her exact words, but they went something like this:

"Relax and open your mind and give yourself freely."

I responded, "Yes."

"Are you ready to let the dimensions open?"

"Yes."

"Can the points of touch be used to release your essence?"

"Yes," I replied.

She started touching different parts of my body by what felt like were only her fingertips. The sensation of her touch was cold and wet. She continued touching me as she talked in a soft slow voice, asking me more questions followed by my answers of "Yes". This proceeded for about 30 minutes, while the entire time she was touching parts of my body. Then abruptly she told me that the Grays were here. I could not see either her or them since I was still lying face down. Eve then started touching me again, starting at the top of my back. It felt like there were little wet dots being placed all over my back in some sort of pattern. It was still very cold in the room with what seemed like a cloud of mist hovering over me.

She told me to relax and to let all of us begin to take the

next step. Then she asked, "Are you ready, and do you have unconditional love?" I replied, "Yes." She started working at my heart from my back side, moving her fingers in a circular pattern over the area. They felt light yet enjoyable as they touched at different points of my body. I was becoming quite comfortable. About 15 minutes went by, and then my right leg started to tighten up like it was cramping. The pain from it was getting worse and worse. I mentioned to her what was happening, and she replied that they were working on something and were releasing whatever it was through my leg. The touches on my heart and down my spine were getting more frequent, still following some sort of pattern. She then said, "Let go of the flow of love." I again responded, "Yes" to her. The pain subsided and I felt a warm sensation in my body. She stated I was now ready and to please turn over. I complied with a "Yes."

Slowly turning over, the towel remained in place. I wasn't sure why, but I did not look around the room. Eve asked me to remain laying face up and covered my eyes with a small towel. Still in a somewhat trance-like state I responded with a "Yes". Now sensing there were three or four beings present at that moment, I felt my arms being touched in different areas, and then down my chest and around my heart. It felt as if I were only being touched by the tips of fingers. The sensations of being touched continued down to my abdomen. She then proceeded to lift the towel over my right leg, moving downward as I felt the touching. She replaced the towel and did the same to my left leg.

I felt very comfortable and yet very vulnerable. Still I could not see anything, but all my other senses were heightened. Slowly the towel was removed from my body, and now I was totally naked. At this point, I think they took my DNA. Eve said, "Very well," and I responded the same "Yes". She told me she was going to leave the room and to get dressed.

I was fully dressed when she came back to the room, and we talked for about half an hour. She told me that everything went very well, but there may be more work to do, that there was something they were not sure about inside. She wanted me to come back in exactly one week and meet again in the same place. Once again I said, "Yes" and then left.

One week later, we were back together. I had been thinking about what had happened and may occur this time. I wanted to be spiritually prepared this time, calling in my guides for protection, making me more aware of what may lie ahead. This session was very different, not at all like before. Eve left the room like before I stripped down and was again naked. There was a really odd feeling to the room. Laying face down on the table again, I was covered by a towel. She said nothing and didn't ask any questions. At this time I sensed she was looking for something within me. It was pain and its release. This time the touch was painful. I kept thinking about my angels and guides watching over me and holding them close in my thoughts. I wanted to understand this whole experience and was willing to do whatever was needed. I didn't know what to expect; the feeling was mostly in pain in my shoulders and neck.

Eve looked at and probed each muscle and joint, not

touching my heart this time. She instructed me to turn over onto my back and proceeded to cover my eyes once again with the towel. She removed the towel, and I was exposed completely to her. Again she took some DNA. She told me to get dressed and left the room. When she came back, she said that our energies were not the same and that we (her and the Grays) would never be in contact with me again. "Leave us in peace and never come back," she said. Replying, I said, "I understand, and may you have peace and joy too." That was it, and I never had another encounter with possible extraterrestrials. Was it real, or not? I am not sure. It was definitely an experience. It truly happened. I hope what you have just read does not offend you in any way. That is not my intent. I did contact Evie Lorgen about what had happened. She said that this was probably very real and I was abused by this sick woman and that this was an encounter.

Starseeds

Many of the people of this planet are not of this world. Their origin and who they are deep within their souls are not from the planet called Earth. They come from all over the universe to share in the experience of what it's like to be human and have a body like ours. Many beings have never known what it's like to feel love, hate, pain, greed, or even death. There are so many reasons some of us are here. Some of us have been here a long time and had many embodiments. This is an experimental world. Have you ever thought to yourselves, why we are so far from the other worlds and galaxies? The reason is very clear: we were to evolve on our own without being influenced by outside events.

Each one of us should ask ourselves if we really fit in to this world we share. I'm sure some of you will feel as I do that this life feels strange and seems odd. Maybe you're a Starseed too. A Starseed is a being of light energy of another vibration and dimension from another part of the universe. You may or may not look anything like what your human body looks like now. Don't be shocked or freak out. Your home world could be anywhere, and how you appear there is not important right now. You have a spirit or soul within you. That's what we all should understand and share. Learning from your life experiences here will help you know yourself better and maybe even help your home world someday when you return. The mansion worlds I speak of are places to share those experiences to either come back to this world or go beyond and pass on in your journey to another new place or go back to where you came from. This planet was created to be where it is in the Universe. Which kinds of beings and living creatures who can interact was also chosen and created. This world is not by chance. We didn't just appear from nothing. As many scientists have said, we are stardust. Many of us are from places you can't even imagine. But you can visit them or know about them. We can travel or visit in dreams, visions, or out-of-body experiences.

We are all connected to everything. The Planet Earth, our sun, and the entire Universe have a connection to us all. You can feel it, deep inside your being and know it's true. We live and breathe stardust every moment of our lives. Everything we touch, see, or hear is Stardust and is spiritual. Open your eyes to that thought and awaken your being to what really is. Smile and enjoy being a human being sharing the experience of living in this world, with love, hope, and caring. Then share it with someone else.

Attachment

We live on a very special planet we call earth. It is dangerous place to experience life. Most of us live our lives just trying to get through the day. We all need to make a paycheck, buy food and have a place to sleep and find shelter. It is hard to concentrate on anything else. There must be more to life than just that all the time, isn't there? Where is your focus in this life? If you are always thinking about and manifesting the need for a paycheck, gas, food or housing, you are focusing on the outer you. You are not looking inside at your inner self. All real change happens when you manifest from the inside. Let us look at that for a moment.

What if you tried turning all of your thoughts within? What would you want to put inside the voided area of your being? Imagine all the things you had inside are gone. What kinds of things do you really want, desire and need? We manifest our lives on a daily basis. Your life and mine are consumed with those attachments. We want certain people, places and things in our lives. It is a form of ownership. Can you imagine clearing yourself of ownership and attachment to anything? Everything you see in this world will turn to dust someday. Manifest only that which you can keep inside of you. If you really want to do this and be free, you must not be left wanting. The kind of things that can be kept inside are the emotions of life. The feeling of peace, calmness, compassion, harmony, and many different kinds of love.

Whatever you want and desire leads to its being fulfilled. What you tell yourself in this world and even in the next will happen. It will manifest, and you will experience it. That is how earth, the mansion worlds and beyond work. Your manifesting does not stop the second you die and pass into the next realm of light vibration. I will say it again: Do not be left wanting. This is a great time to fulfill or discard thoughts and desires you may have in life. Some examples of this are more connections of places, things and people. You want to visit or live in a certain part of the world. I have to own a home with 3 bedrooms and be near the ocean. I want a person sexually to do this with me. All are desires and they may cause you to come back to another life to fulfill them. Do those desires now or discard them from your being. If you do manifest fulfill them and enjoy every moment of your desires.

I also have the same experience of being on the planet earth as you do. My thoughts and desires are unique to me. Yours are unique to you. No two people have the same ones all the time. There are many that we manifest as a group, and all of those will come to pass in some way. We cause war, famine and all kinds of disasters as a group. We also do great and wonderful things. Let us move all our minds and bodies with the thought of a positive world of peace. Then there will be peace. Many on this planet are doing just that.

One of the issues of being human is it has become habit forming. We are addicted to manifesting the world the way it is. We are fulfilling our group desires. Many want money or what it can do for them. Want things so badly that you can feel the desire with you. You can actually feel it physically.

You must ask yourself these questions: Can I stop a desire or what I want? Can I stop what others desire or want? You may not be able to do that. It is easy and yet is very hard. Changing your focus changes your life. Are you ready for that kind of change? The other issue is what have you already learned in this life. What has your environment or genetics given you? Some things you are going to experience just because of the place you were born or the family you have been given. You choose to come to this planet. You chose your parents and some of the life you live. It was manifested before you got here. You will fulfill some of those desires you have chosen to fulfill, those things you will have a hard time changing.

Does that mean you should not try? No! You must go within and change what you can. The best thing is to experience life to the fullest. It is your life, and no one else in this world manifests it for you. Your desires and needs are all yours. You can choose what you want or not want. Freedom of choice is within you. If you really have a desire, go out and fulfill it. No regrets and no wishing you did. That just leads to more attachment. You will do what you desire someday. It will happen in this life or the next. Many die or pass on to the next realm and regret something they did not do. They may even come back to this planet again just to do that one thing. My desire is for you to enjoy this life. Do all you want and desire to make you happy and fulfilled. You can say to yourself: "Wow that was a great life and I did it all." That is how I feel within myself every day.

Visions: Past-Future

Visions are in the eye of the beholder. You see through yourself the images and the interpretation of them. They are deciphered, categorized, dissected and judged by the person seeing them. You may try not to do any of those things but you do them without thinking. As a human being it happens all of the time. As I write certain things down, it is through my point of view and my understanding. You are reading my interpretation and view. Then forming your own feeling and view of what you are reading.

I had a vision the other night. It started quickly, then it came over me, and I was in a trance-like state. It lasted about two to three hours, not stopping until the very end. Some of it was about the past, some about the future of life on this planet. When it will happen is dependent on the energy here. As the vision began, I set my mind to recall it later. Saying to myself, "This may be something to remember. There is a season for all." Now I knew I would recall it and was ready to see what was before me.

There did not seem to be any patterns of when, where or why I was going. They had happened so fast one right after another and I just wrote them down as I remembered them.

The first vision came, and I was with a group of people. Maybe there were five to seven of them. We were sitting in some kind of vehicle not like anything I could describe. All of us were watching the lights moving around us, and then we stopped at a spot that looked a little like a road. In front of us was a city full of life. Many buildings and structures seemed to be moving, moving people and things. Many massive blocks were crossing over and under each other. It looked a little like our freeway system here. Larger buildings were off in the distance. We got in closer and pulled up a short distance from where the main area of the city was. A very large crane-like machine was lifting blocks to place in another area. It seemed very busy and life was going on everywhere.

Then all of sudden, the area we were in started to shake very strongly all around us. We were not affected at all. It was as though we were there and not part of it. All the people were running and starting to scream. All the buildings and structures were crumbling before our eyes. I could tell it was an earthquake, and it was happening right in front of us. Some of the buildings were now collapsing, and you could see the terror in the faces of the people running. Just to our right side there was a tall, black obelisk, and it was now moving like a pendulum back and forth, starting to break off and then it does, landing right on top of some people running below us.

All of us in the vehicle realized people were dying, and our eyes were wide open. We saw all forms of debris falling around us. We all saw a city being leveled to the ground. There were people being hurt and others trying to find a safe place to hide. There were even some people trying to save others. It looked as if three out of every four people were hurt or dying. Everyone around us was being affected. You could feel the pain and suffering. A sense of caring moved over us as we sat watching, knowing there was nothing we could do to stop it or help the city that had collapsed as we were not really there. We were only there to see it up close and personal. Then it was over, and back into the light we went.

Looking at this event and the experience was very moving and emotional. Having been through many earthquakes here in California, they were nothing like that one, so up close and personal. Thousands of people were dying, and we watched as the city came to an end. The feeling I had was of something from our past. This had happened a long time ago and we saw it happen. It was a powerful experience.

Quickly, the next visions appeared, and they were about the future. It sort of looked like a collage of events one right after another.

Humans are about to change their evolutionary being. We have many limits, and many of those limits will stop. I do not know when this will happen or how some of it will unfold.

Let us talk about cloning and the current technology of reproducing an animal of the past or one currently living. This has opened the door to new thoughts and ideas of what we can do. These visions are what are coming. We will understand how life is created at the cell level, and we will start to create life. Some are going to be new kinds and some old ones too. The DNA strand will totally be understood and begin to be manipulated.

We will start to create humans in a new image, eliminating flaws and changing the DNA pattern. The rich will get this opportunity first; then slowly, it will flow down to the masses.

You will no longer die from old age, and you will not die from disease. People will start to live to hundreds of years of age. The only way life will end will be self-inflicted, an accident or a disaster.

A new type of blood will be created that will enhance and change our bodies. It will make us into a new kind of woman and man. Some of us will do the change easily, while others will fight it and stay with their old blood. Those will die off.

You will even be able to choose the kind of body you desire. People will remain almost ageless. Sounds like fiction? It will be a fact and it will happen. But wait, there is more.

Brain engineering will happen too. The brain will be understood and expanded. We will get beyond the current 7-10% we use now and get to almost 60-70% of usage. Because of these changes in us and our understanding, we will seriously start exploring our universe. Our bodies now are affected by being in space for long periods of time, yet that will end with our new blood and bodies that can last longer. Space travel is going to happen on a really large scale. We will start to go to the stars, see new galaxies and beyond.

Gravity will also be fully understood. We will be able to move things easily. Light and vibration will be used to communicate. Our theories of how creation began with a big bang will end. We live in a plasma universe, and science will have a new set of theories to explain how things began.

Humans will still have petty problems, such as moral, political and choosing our leaders among ourselves. We will be one planet yet still divided on many subjects. The discoveries of science will change us all. People have said that "ONCE A ROCK STARTS GOING DOWN A HILL, IT IS VERY HARD TO STOP AN AVALANCHE". Science will start that rock for humankind.

Many discoveries will be made, revealing ancient ruins of our past on this earth. We have been here longer than we thought. We were also more evolved too. We will have to look at our history of what we thought we were.

Wars will break out, and terrorists will strike. Even nuclear weapons will be used. One will be used on the United States of America, and a city will be destroyed. I see the fall of China, the U.S. and all the major countries. There will be people who have everything and others who have nothing. There will be a time where food will be gone or just a little left. There will be no money; just an exchange of kindness or trades to get by. Out of all this disaster will come the change of Humanity.

Our planet will shift and change its movement. The moon will shift, and weather patterns will change. The people of earth will have moral and political options and will need to decide. The disasters will bring us together and prepare us for change.

Then this vision came to an end, and I had to put together my thoughts, trying to write down as much as I could remember. It may seem a little all over the place and not very organized. Anyone reading this must understand how hard it is to see something and then try to write it down clearly. This was my most difficult of all the visions I have had and tried to capture on paper.

This vision was very emotional for me and a real mixing of future events. I am not sure what will come first or even last. I have just written it down as I understood it. You have to think in terms of life, death and the experience of it all. Many on this planet will not deal with these changes. They will fight, and they will die. They will be crying for their god and praying with their religious beliefs. Some will be concerned about their countries or even their race: White, Black, Hispanic, Asian and others.

All of this will fail. The rock will fall and change will happen. Change will bring new ideas, thoughts and a whole new set of problems: The trials of putting a planet of people back together and how they look at their existence.

As we expand our understanding of the universe, we will experience great successes and great tragedies. Millions of people will die as we go forth. Earth is just a place to dwell in and learn who we truly are inside. My hope is for humans to work together to make a better place for all. My hope is for us to all join hands for a better life within for all of us.

It is just a few steps from becoming a reality. Prepare yourself and accept what will be. You can be a part of the caring group or choose have self interest. The choice is yours. All life is precious, and everyone deserves a life of understanding and caring. Make the change within today.

The Present

Many new age people around the world believe in what they call "living in the now". That always sounds so easy to do just live and experience it. However, that most people live in the past or future is more accurate. I had a friend years ago help me to better understand this concept. He knows who he is, and if he is reading this, he would not want his name mentioned. He had many great teachings for me over the years.

I want you to sit down or you can stand, and put your hand upright in front of you where you can see it. Picture in your mind an old book you read many years ago. It is now in your hand again. You see the title and remember what is inside of it. You are now thinking in the past and you are living old memories within. Yet, they are now in the present. We do the same kind of thing when we drive a car and look through the rear view mirror. We are looking at what is behind us.

The same can be said about the future ahead of us. Take out your hand and put it in front again. Think of something you want to have in your life and imagine it is in your hand now. Your thoughts go to desires of how you will get the thing in front you. All of your focus is now there, and you are not living in the present.

Most of us do this all of time, always thinking about what happened in the past or what might be in the future. We worry about things that really do not matter.

Always say to yourself. "I AM IN THE NOW". You can be manifesting all that you desire as if you already have what you want in your life. The desires will appear and events will happen. This really works, and your life will change. You are no longer living in the past or the future.

Time

There really is no time, only just this moment. We are the ones that give definition to time. Every occurrence is in the moment and is what we make of it. All the memories we have inside exist and change as we change. Updating or reorganizing them, we look at them with new eyes to determine what was important, what really happened and why. Every time a memory comes to us we do this. It is our belief and point of view. It keeps us balanced and rational in our thoughts. Our minds and thoughts are a wonderful gift to us.

We deal with many different events in our lives. Disasters, death, trauma, praise, success, happiness and love are part of the human experience. How we organize and give them meaning is important to who we are inside. It can make us happy or sad, and the choice is ours. The human experience of life is ours to live each moment. The planets, stars and galaxies move to give us some sort of thought of time. Our bodies change and we feel older as years pass by. Life on Earth is a blink of the eye in time. We see it and experience that moment and then we become something else. Enjoy the time you give yourself here. See, feel and understand what it is to be human.

Human History

Ruins exist all over the world that depict the history of humans, what we have built over many centuries and left to the next generations. Many have been found and tested to determine how long ago they were built. The issue with testing has been clouded by religious judgment. Some ruins in Egypt are much older than their testing dates. Most religions believe that humans have only been here six or seven thousand years. At least, that is what their doctrine says from their books of truth from the gods. Not that religion is wrong, as most came from some real truth. Religious leaders made the meaning their own and expanded it to control others.

Science has done some of the same with their theories of how things work. Some theories are formed just to fit what the scientist believes. I will give you an example of that kind of thinking. The science of today believes in a "Big Bang Theory" of creation of the universe. We can look into the past with light 13 billion years ago. Science thinks that because of men like Albert Einstein saying that formulas like E=MC2 are the foundation of the universe, there had to have been a big bang to cause the universe to expand and be what it is today. The truth is it is a theory and it is wrong. Many parts are correct in the formula itself, just not that part. We live in a plasma universe where 99% of the universe is made up of plasma. It is the fourth element of matter. Our sun is made of plasma.

The reason I am mentioning history, religion and science is that we have been misled through many years of lies and misdirection to the real truths of humankind. We have been a part of this planet hundreds of thousands of years. Some of the ruins here are from our long distance past and are part of who we are now. It is our true history and culture's past monuments to our past.

Much of what has existed on this planet lasts a few thousand years and then turns to dust. Why do we not remember what happened to us? Most of us have lived many times on this planet. Each time we go to the mansion worlds we stay for a space of time. We want to know more, so many have chosen to come back again to learn something not learned the last time. Every time we come back to this planet we put on a veil or cloud of memory loss. It keeps us focused on learning whatever we were choosing to learn this time. If we saw all the lifetimes we have had, it would confuse us daily. So we do not remember them.

Now, I have been here many times too, 57 times to be exact. Many people have seen their records of their past lives or at least part of them, as I have seen 3 of mine fully. I have seen them in the hall of records in the Mansion Worlds. You can see yours too if you desire in your travels.

Chemistry

The code of the chemistry of the universe is living plasma. The universe, our bodies and every cell that exists came from the same place. We are all one and are part of the expansion of creation. There is never anything that dies, it just changes the form of that creation. All people and objects move from one form to another and then on to the next. It is truly beautiful. We are beautiful too in how we interact with all of the energies that exist. We feel the flow of energy-to-energy connections.

All of my life has been part of that energy flow, and so has yours. When we lay our bodies down in the final end of our lives here on this planet, we will change into new energy. Look up at the stars, moon and planets, and see part of yoursel in the sky above. The planet we live on is part of us too. We are always connected to all of it, and it connects back to us. One of the best things about being human is learning to truly connect on a deep and meaningful way with all. Awake and arrive at the understanding that all is connected. We are one and you can see the beauty of it. Every moment of our lives we feel the flow of energy through and all around all of us.

The past, the present and the future are one too. Think about all that exists from one little atom to entire galaxies. Each cell can be aware of being one. The natural law of the universe is expansion of awareness.

Love is a word that means many things and in itself is expressed in so many ways. You can love all from one tiny cell of existence to the overall love for everything. You helped to create and are part of creation. My heart is open to feeling it deeply inside. My thoughts, your thoughts, the planets and the universe itself were created to feel, hear and see. It is you and you are one.

The Internet

Our world is changing very rapidly, and the Internet is doing that on a global scale. The real interaction between people everywhere is less and less. Everywhere you go you see people looking at their computers, cell phones or e-books. They have given up their personal lives of touching each other's soul and experiencing their lives to a screen that feeds them in a new way. You can get a connection to others through the Internet only if you focus intent within yourself and express it back to the universe.

Everything is spiritual through the connection of our thoughts and desires. We judge what we see, hear and feel inside and send out energy for everyone to share. Collectively, we are all sharing all that the Internet is expressing. Individually, we are getting addicted to this form of connection. What we look at changes how our thoughts fit into this new world of cyberspace. We look at words and images of others and can also hear the sounds of all who are now connected to it. Meanings that are expressed are of views that we may never have thought of before. Are they the original intent? No, they are what we see and hear through our own point of view. It opens us up yet limits us too.

One image on the Internet could have thousands of meanings. The real meaning of the one who put that image there is expanded or diminished, and it good or bad depending on the individual receiving it. Our minds have been opened to the new, and we have lost much of the innocence of life. We are seeing or hearing all the good and happiness in the world, and we also see or hear all the sadness and despair. It is now up close and in our lives; it is truly what we are addicted to. We want it and just cannot stop looking for more of it. It is another way of limitation and escape and not going within.

Movies have also been a form of escape for the last hundred years. We escape into a world of images for a few hours. They are living pictured dreams and visions of others where anything is possible even the impossible. We immerse ourselves in a fantasy of a different life other than the one we are living. There are moments in each film that touch us inside. We see or hear something that is a connection of relating and insight. We often experience emotions watching these images and sounds. Tears, fear, happiness and joy can happen as we watch.

Over time we have learned what kind of images we enjoy and like to experience. The Internet is similar to the kind of interaction we have with movies. Do we like drama, comedy, adventures or love stories? All are available to anyone who wants to receive them. The question to look at is this: What do we want with this and why does it attract us? Perhaps it is because it gives us experiences and feelings, some good, some bad. The choice is ours to go and see what happens with this insight and what we desire.

Our Leaders

All governments come and then go as time passes in this world. What happens to our leaders? Many have ruled and fallen away back into history. No institution ever lasts. The question is: "How do they rule?" Do they do it with the right intent? Are they working to make lives better or is it more about control?

We live in a world with those who have and those who do not. Our world could feed, shelter and love everyone, yet we know that it never has. Why is this? Should not everyone have a decent experience of life, liberty and the pursuit of happiness? How many people have died or suffered so others may live well? Many live their lives well beyond what they need to survive. Is it greed and power that feeds them?

I have heard that 1% of the people run the world, having most of the money. I believe there is more to it than that. The leaders of our society, the doctors and lawyers along with the media, control everything. If they genuinely cared for every one of us, life on planet earth would be different. We are afforded health care that does not heal and is merely used for politic purposes, talking of curing diseases, yet never really doing anything to further the cause. The media tells us only what the people in charge want us to know and control us on a massive scale.

If the doctors, lawyers and media did honestly care, the world would be a different place. Not just in a few years, but it would happen right now. This planet could truly be for all the people of the world. We could provide food, shelter and love to everyone. Here in the U.S. it is the same. We say it is the land of the free, but this is a lie, it is not free. We are all in bondage and are being used. We get little spoonfuls of hope for a better life, while being divided through the media asking us to choose sides of any argument. These are not true leaders, and they will fall over time.

Suicide

Did you know that over 250,000 people in China commit suicide every year? In the United States someone does it every 17 minutes. In Canada it is even worse, and in the modern countries it is one of the top five ways to die. The number one way to kill yourself is by hanging. More women do this than men, and the men are better at doing it. If someone fails they are more likely to try again later.

Why do we as humans keep trying to do this? Is it lack of money, food, shelter or water or just that no one cares for them? They are the forgotten ones and feel they have nothing to hold them here. In the homeless or mentally ill the numbers are even higher. They experience despair, depression and an imbalance of their thoughts.

There are others who want to take life too, that is, of others rather than themselves. Killers feel that taking a life gives them some power. How many can I take with me as I die? This happens all over the world. Maybe it gives their lives meaning. Maybe some want to be famous or known as a martyr for a cause. Will I be remembered? What will shock my world, my family or my friends?

I believe we could stop almost all of these tragedies. All we really have to do is care. It is again about who is in charge of the power. It is about life, not money.

Healing the World

If we want to heal the world, we need to start with the individual, just one person saying they want to help. We need to change the government, and we need to communicate our needs to these millionaires, billionaires and others in control. We need to talk to the doctors, lawyers and the media. People everywhere need to stand up and say, "NO MORE!". No more death. No more greed. Let us all save the world or at least try to do something each day to better our lives. Make this promise to yourself: "I will help others every day for the rest of my life." You want to help others, not because someone else tells you too but because it is right.

"Pay it forward," "Can't we all just get along?" "Love one another." These are all simple phrases that everyone knows. This is what we should be saying every morning. You should thank the creator of all and say you are glad to be here. Then stop and ponder or meditate within. How can I help the world today? How can I help others? Step outside and really observe the beauty around you. This is a special planet and you are part of that experience. Get your mind ready to do something positive and useful.

Be open to change, and look inside your heart as you find

someone you can help today. When you see them or find them, truly help! Give them the caring and love that is inside you. If we were all to do this each day, the world would change. Lives would be saved and others would live happier lives. And the people you help today; tell them to do the same thing. Spread the thought of helping others. If you teach another how to help others, it will keep on going. If you have the experience and of caring, then you should show others how to do it.

The change will happen, and one by one it will make a difference. We can have a world of peace, harmony and love. It will not always be perfect, and it will fail sometimes. But overall, the world will be a better place because of you. I thank you, honor you and give you my love if will just do this each day. This is what I do every day and will for the rest of my life. It starts with me making the choice.

Help the sick, the mentally ill, the homeless or those who are depressed, and give them some of your caring. Give them hope and the love you have inside. Even if you have nothing tangible to give, you can give a hug, or a shoulder to cry on or a hand to hold. Just seeing a smile or a look of love in your eyes helps. We all have these things to share. Give them freely, often and with passion. The people you can help are everywhere, and all you have to do is look around. You will see them, and you will tell them you care. When the day is done and you go to sleep at night say, "Thank you" for being available and to help others.

Suffering and Pain

Why is there so much suffering and pain in this world? I have asked this question many times. I work with people daily who have illnesses and constant pain, and I use my energy to ease the suffering they feel. I have discovered the truth to why suffering happens and why some healing does not work.

Some people came here to this world to experience pain and suffering. They chose it and are living it each day of their lives. It is part of the human experience for all of us. There is not one person who has not felt some kind of pain. It is just that some have much more than others.

It can also depend on where you were born and the family you chose to be with. Each continent has a different experience. When you look at Africa, the Middle East, China, Europe or the American continents, you can see how all are so different in the lifestyles of the inhabitants. Because each experience is so different, you may not understand how the suffering happens. Cultures of despair and poverty can impact the pain and suffering. The choices you made before you came into this life impact the level of your pain and suffering as well.

You also need to look at the ones not in pain or suffering. What is their experience? They can watch what happens to others or help. Pain and suffering are everywhere and are all part of the human experience. What do you do when you see the pain or suffering of others? You have choices, and it is up to you to decide what you will do. Will you look away and do nothing? Will you help in some way? If we choose to help we need to think about: Why am I doing this? How much help can I offer? Will it really help? We learn and understand ourselves and our world through helping others with their pain and suffering.

This understanding leads to caring. You start to care for others and yourself more. That is what expands the universe, the energy of caring. It is why we suffer and have pain, so we can all expand our energy of caring.

If you want to know God or know yourself completely, you must care. Some people use the word love, which has many meanings and is a form of caring. When you care about something, you move energy. What you care about is important, and the focus of it can be seen, heard or felt. The world needs to care about the people, animals, plants and the planet itself. We need to care about our place in the universe. We need to care about our connection to all that is. We are all connected, and we are one.

Fear

Fear or the image of fear sometimes looks like a reality in life. The unknown scares us. But fear is not real. You give it an image, and that gives it life.

Fear can burn within you. No one causes you to feel that way. You do this to yourself. Step back and see it for what it is. Let fear go, and have no fear inside your being. Let go of past, present or future fears. They are not real. Just experience life without judgment, and let things flow as they should. Be calm and at peace. No one can really hurt you inside. Only you can hurt yourself with fear.

The World Today

How we see the world today is so much different than how it was, say 100 years ago. People are so busy and full of life. People are doing all kinds of things, many that you and I are not even aware of. The animals of our planet are living and surviving, just being what they are meant to be. The plants of our planet grow, wither and die, then come back next season to be reborn again.

We have a planet that spins and changes daily. Our sun glows with power and energy giving the earth warmth. Each day the ocean rolls in and out with the tides as the moon dances above. Water evaporates into the atmosphere, and as rain comes back to the ground. The electromagnetic field of our world energizes all that lives and dies. As I watch all the stars each night in a dance of life, I see as part of all of us, and we are part it too. I love to embrace the joy it brings my heart.

Each day I stop every so often for a moment and ponder it all. Then I realize we are in a very special place, a world of great beauty. Looking all around moves me inside. My heart fills with energy when I look at a sunrise or sunset and see the colors glow for me. When I watch the clouds move across the sky and the plants glow as the wind brushes against them.

I take the world into my life like a sponge. Nature is so beautiful, and you have knowledge that you are here to experience it. We are all here for a reason that most do not understand. Take a moment to breathe and connect with the experience of your life. You are having a great experience of life, and it is wonderful to be here.

I am so thankful to be here at this time and in this moment. It is and always will be special to me. We are all part of life, and it is good.

Section II

Spiritual Learning Rituals

Just a Few Thoughts

I am not part of any religion or group. Not to say that I will not be someday. So far it is not for me and my experience in this world. Having studied almost all of the religions, each one is good if you feel joy, peace and happiness being there. So be it for you. There is good in all.

For me, I love the feeling of all life. Every single molecule and cell that exists is alive with energy. I believe that nothing is dead. A table is made of dead wood. Or is it? Energy is living and always moving. We may not see or hear how atoms and cells move together or push away. They have connection within. The air that we breathe is alive with energy. If you understand, feel it and enjoy it, let it, be part of your life.

There is a story everyone knows: "The Story of the Glass of Water". Is the glass half full or is it half empty? It is a point of view. Change your view and change your life. Life is always full. Drink it up, so you may feel the flow run through you, changing who you are inside.

Important Information to Know

There are certain ideas for you to know and understand about soul traveling. These are things very important. Do not travel without remembering them.

1. Discernment and Point of View. You are seeing through your eyes, your knowledge, your experiences, and you are reflecting in your mind what is going on around you.
2. No Judgment. Let things be what they are. No right or wrong, they just exist as is.
3. No Fear. You are the only one who causes you that feeling inside.
4. Enjoy all your experiences. They are for you.
5. Just because you see something, or experience it does not mean you must tell everyone or even one other person. It is for you, and only you. How many religions have started like this? Not everyone will understand. Tell only those you feel led to tell.

So, now you are ready to travel. I am ready too, so let us begin.

Exploring

Traveling or "exploring" as I like to call it takes focus, yet sometimes it takes lack of focus. The first part is to focus on your thoughts. Ask yourself: "What kinds of learning or exploring do I need?" You are the only one who knows. It may be hard to get ideas or a feeling of what you need inside. What realms you go to are a reflection of you and your needs. Who you see, how you feel, what you hear, and with whom you interact is all part of the experience. You may need to feel comfortable or have a guide to help you make the choice. For me, I just have a thought, and I am on my journey exploring.

The observer mode is a life understanding experience. You see others and their interactions, one's many inner conflicts of "Human against Human". Their thoughts are looking outward and not inward. This happens with generation after generation. We pass down of habits, rituals and perceptions of what is real. The mansion worlds provide a good learning center for growth and understanding. It can also be a stumbling block to overcome. The reason the mansion worlds exist is to help humans overcome themselves, that is, when we think we have arrived and know it all, the limitation of growth occurs.

There is so much more beyond these worlds, and they are

nice to visit and interact with. Always stay in your mind and in your spirit. I believe it is a great to see, hear and visit the mansion worlds. But always seek more, strive to know what there is and look further in exploring. It will be worth your thoughts and growth. You can visit these places to see beyond with no limits, no stopping. Let us explore together.

Beyond, the realms of light and darkness are waiting for you. You will visit places where there are no beings around you. You will be alone in places with or without form. There are so many, they are without number. And there are other beings out there too. Some look like us, and others do not. Life is everywhere. We are not alone in this wonderful gift of life.

Keep your thoughts of wonder open to change. What you think now, may not apply to what you see and hear in your travels. It changes and so do you. You have to want the change and desire it within, to need it. Then put your focus to go. In a short time, you will be there just like I have been. Have no fear of the unknown. It is all known; you just have not experienced it yet. Be here, in the now, in the present, and let it unfold. See the vision of existence. You and I are eternal. We are one.

How to Travel and Explore

Step 1: Basic Travel

Have you ever been in a really dark room? I mean a really dark. No light at all. Close your curtains. Put up blankets or towels over them. Tape up or block any doors, and turn off all lights. You are now in the dark. Slowly look around the room. You see nothing. But wait, in about five or 10 minutes you will start to see the outlines of objects in the room. In half an hour, you will see the whole room. You may have done a good job of blocking the light out, so it may take a little longer. You will still see everything in the room. Your eyes have adjusted to the light and vibration of the room.

The same thing happens when you go from darkness to bright light only it is a faster adjustment. It still takes a few minutes when you step into full light. Both the light and darkness are one extreme of the other in the each of the realms. Many of the realms or worlds do not know the other ones exist. Some of them do know, helping the other ones in their growth and understanding. All of the places are like this with light and darkness.

When you adjust your eyes, you are in fact adjusting your vibration. Each place you go to, you will adjust to that vibration. Because I have been into photography, it has provided my insight into light and dark. You need to know the detailed measures of light. To put an image on unexposed film or a memory card is the same. You must expose it to the light. You may ask, "How much light?"

On a camera you have a shutter. It opens and closes very quickly. That is where your light comes from. If you just open the shutter and expose the film or card, what do you get? A blurred spot of light, that is all. All you see is the light. There is no adjustment. Even if you slow the shutter down or make it faster, the result is the same. It is still a blurred image.

You may ask: "How do I get an image?" There is something on a camera called an aperture. It is an opening that is very small or very large. It is a hole that is round. The number 1 is a large opening, 2 is a little smaller, 3 is even smaller still. There is a 4, 5 and 6, and they are even smaller. How does this help the image of what you see? You may think you should just open it all the way to let in the most light. The hole number 1 is the largest, and there needs to be a balance of light. You balance the shutter with the aperture. The bigger the opening, the faster the shutter should be. That is the adjustment. That is the control of light. This is really important. What are you hoping to see?

What is fun about this is when you do the different setting and balance the light, you can see the images. When you adjust the aperture this what happens:

1. If you look at a flower you can see it and the person and the mountain in the background are blurred.
2. If you look at the person, you may see the flower and the person, but the mountain is still blurred.
3. When you look at the mountain, you may see the flower, the person and the mountain.

Here is the next thing you have to do. All the images are there. They are still blurred and not in focus. There is a ring on a camera, and you have to focus it. When you focus it, all becomes clear.

You may be asking: "How does this apply to traveling or exploring?" Let me explain.

a. You are the film and its memories.
b. Your body is the box or camera.
c. The door that opens your mind is the shutter.
d. Your point of view is the aperture.
e. How you discern or understand life is your focus.

You are a great and wonderful camera of experiences. Are you are ready to explore yourself? Ready to be open to see what is out there? You must direct your inner camera in to the right direction. How? Everyone and every camera has a view finder. Look about you right now. Where are you? How did you get to that spot and this moment? Your eyes see what is around you. Close your eyes and you shall see. You are now looking through the view finder. Picture something in your mind. The shutter opens. Look around and you are using your aperture. Pick out one thing and get closer. Now you have the focus and discernment of what you see.

Travel is that easy. Travel is that fast. Now we should look at the next step. Are you ready?

Step 2: Hearing and Movement

Have you ever looked at something and did not know what it was or maybe you were not sure what it was. What you were seeing did not make any sense to you. I want you to think of learning something new without judgment. You have to totally accept it at face value. No right or wrong. Take a chance and flow with my thoughts.

When traveling and exploring realms of light, and are you sitting where you are right now? Close your eyes to see. Look and travel as if you are the camera. Look and observe your surroundings. Now I want you to think of a video camera. Wow! Moving pictures and the pictures have sound. You can hear what you see. Listen to what is around you. Do you hear anything? You might hear wind, water or other sounds. Here is the good part of this. Sit down where you are, be very still and listen all around you. Hear what you are hearing. Find where the sound is coming from, and get even closer to what you see. Can you see it and hear it? Do this as a game. Go here and go there. But do not touch anything. It may seem hard, yet it gets easier with practice. You are now traveling in the observer mode. What you see has sound and moving pictures. It is that easy. It is that fast. Let us go to the next step.

Step 3: Finding a Friend

Travel has so much freedom to it. No bounds or limits unless you give it some. Have you looked at something even deeper than before, heard it and still did not know what it was you were looking at? It did not make any sense. Sometimes you need help to understand.

I want you to sit down and clear your thoughts. Close your eyes and picture a person right in front of you. They can be standing or sitting. They can be anyone you wish. But, this time I want you to think of someone very special. This person is your friend and has been with you for a long time. He or she is your personal guide. They are right in front of you right now. They exist to help and instruct you. I am sure they are happy to be there for you. Every moment of your life they have been guiding and loving you. Can you picture them in front of you now? Think of them and say, "Yes". Look at them with your mind's eye. Notice how they are looking at you too. Do you see the love they have in their eyes for you? Can you feel their love? This is a very special moment for both of you.

Now comes the truly good part of this experience. This is one of my favorite moments in my life. Would you like to talk with your guide? You can, right now! You are there, and so is your guide. I want you now to ask a few easy questions. Listen to the small soft voice that is there. I am going to give you three questions to ask your guide. You can pick one or all three, the choice is yours. You can ask them in your mind or out loud. Either way is okay to them. There is no right or wrong way to connect and communicate.

1. Hello, how are you? Listen for the answer.
2. Do you have a name I can call you? Listen for the answer.
3. How long have you been with me? Listen to the answer.

When you are done with the three questions and answers, you may want to think of a few of your own. You can now talk as long as you want or need to. When you are done, say goodbye; yet they will stay with you. They are your guide, and now you have a way to talk with them. They are no longer in front of you now.

You now know who your guide is, and you know their name. You are not alone. They can help you in so many ways. They are one of many of the guides you will meet on your travels and journeys. They are helping you to make sense of what does not make sense. It is that easy. It is that fast. Let us go on to the next step.

Step 4: Travel

Sit down or lie down, and get calm comfortable. Close your eyes and picture a peaceful place in your mind. Your guide is with you. You may see them or you not, but they are there helping you right now. You may feel them or sense their presence. In your mind or say out loud, "I wish and desire to travel right now." Listen to the sounds around you. Hear the wind or energy flowing over you. Your body will remain where it is, while inside you may start to get a feeling. You may feel a rolling kind of motion, a turning or floating. Do not be afraid. You are getting ready to pop out of your body. It is a normal feeling. Remember your guide is with you.

You rise in your spiritual body or as a energy ball of light. At first you may see the room or place you are in right now, while out of your body. That is called astral travel, when you move around in a spirit body and see local current people or places. Now you can move about like that or you can go deeper in motion. That would be soul travel where you have a spiritual cord attached to your human body and your soul's energy being. There is a big difference in the two types of travel.

With both, understand that you are still connected with your body that is laying down. You cannot be harmed in any way. Where do you want to go? Your higher self knows what experiences you should have. Let it guide you. Enjoy this moment and the feelings you are getting. There is nothing else like the feeling of flying or floating.

You may go to any place you wish. The choice is yours. Explore the universe and all of its wonders. It is all waiting for you right now. You can see old friends or make new ones. Learn and understand the deepest insights to your existence. Enjoy the journey, and remember what you experienced.

The time will pass, and you will pop back into your body. That can happen slowly or quickly. Do not be afraid, as it does not hurt. Rest for a second and collect your thoughts. Think to yourself what just happened to you. You can get up and walk around. Write down what happened or just ponder it. It is up to you. It is that easy and that fast. Now let us move on to the next step.

Step 5: Doubt

This is hard for some people, while many will find it easy. This is for your understanding of yourself. You may have doubts about what just happened. Question yourself. Did this really happen? Is this a real experience or just in my mind? Have I lost my mind? All of these are good questions. My answer is that you have not lost your mind. You are spiritual before you are human. You are experiencing who you are inside. You are not the body you have here on this planet. It is a shell you are in at the moment. You just experienced being you, the real you.

My belief is very strong. I must say something that may be hard to grasp or understand. I need you to think about it and ponder. "If you think it, you have done it." You may not have done physically, but you have done it spiritually. Everyone that exists judges themselves. Keep your mind and actions pure to yourself. Be true to yourself and your inner being. Remember there is no right or wrong. It is a hard concept to understand and come to grips with.

I will give you of a few examples of what I mean. This one is about flying and exploring our planet or universe. This is the most common experience almost everyone has. Whether it is astral or soul travel does not matter. I thoroughly enjoy the feeling of lifting off the ground to float. I just lightly push off and go to so many kinds of places. I can fly over the ocean, mountains, buildings or out into space. All of it is fun and exciting.

Another example is that of dying, that is, experiencing

different ways to die. That sounds odd to desire death, but remember there is no right or wrong. I had a time where I wanted to experience being shot by a gun. I was taken to a realm to experience just that. I was walking on a street, and there were others there. They came at me and wanted something I had on me that was in my pockets. I said, "No, it is mine." They pulled out a gun and said to give it to them. I was being robbed, yet again I said, "No". They shot me, and I slowly fell to the ground as if in slow motion. I felt the bullet enter my chest and stop my heart from beating. I was still alive inside and was experiencing it all. I was not frightened. I was totally calm and observed every part of what was happening. I enjoyed the experience and can now say I have experienced being shot and dying. I am happy I did that. You may have had this kind of experience too. Yours may have been different, and you may have had more than one of them. It is part of our journey and learning.

The third example is having sexual encounters. I was in a realm of light, sound and vibration. I went through the open door. There were buildings all around me. They were tall and wide on both sides of the walkway. I seemed to glide over to the one on my right and went in. It was a very large room with many other rooms inside. The people were friendly and were laughing and singing. All were enjoying being together. Two people came over to me and said, "Hi". They asked me if this was my first time here. I said, "Yes, I think it is".

Looking around, it did look familiar. The people asked me if I would like to sit with them or maybe meet some of their friends. They said, "Let us sit down and talk." We all sat down, and as we were talking I was looking around the room and saw a couple. This man and woman were together, and they were not just talking. They were having sex, kissing, touching and much more, yet I was not shocked or uncomfortable. It felt natural. I was calm and even a little excited. I knew I was out of my human body, in a place that was sexually open and free. My being must have wanted the feeling and experience. The female next to me smiled and asked if I would enjoy kissing, and I replied, "Yes." I am not going to give all the details, but this went on for a while. Then I left and came back from my journey.

You may have questions. I did too. "There is sex in the realms of light"? The answer is yes, in some, though not all of them. Many do not engage in any sexual activity. That is the most common. There is affection and caring, just no sex as we have here on this planet. No judgment or right and wrong. Do not feel bad if you have not been to one of these places. Some of us go to them and others do not. It is up to you.

Have you ever had a wet dream? Have you ever had sex with someone who was not your wife or husband? Maybe with someone you never met before? It is okay and it was for your experience. Freedom has its place in the universe and beyond. You set the limits. I believe: "If you think it, you have done it."

These were my examples and my experiences. You may have some of the same experiences or not even close to any of these. They are just examples of what is out there to see and hear. There are so many different realms and worlds to explore.

What is normal to one person is not to another. Your inner being will have to discern what is normal for you. I have my own thoughts on what normal is.

Do not second guess yourself. Be one with who you are. Use these five steps for traveling and exploring. I hope you find them useful. I did. Apply them and see for yourself.

Energy Connections

Let us see ourselves with new eyes. We are beings of light and energy. Within us is constant motion. Let us learn how to tap into this energy within. Everyone knows about their physical bodies. They have a head, arms, feet, heart and blood moving through it all. If you go deeper there are cells and DNA.

There is so much more to our bodies than we can imagine. Many cultures on this planet have known about the energy centers within us. We are already hard wired with energy. We just have to understand how this energy works and what we can do with these energy centers. Most people who know about them call them Chakras. I like the term "energy centers". There are seven basic centers on the body. They are easy to find. They each have a color and a sound vibration.

	LOCATION	COLOR	SOUND
1.	Top of the head	Violet	OM
2.	Third eye (just above the nose)	Indigo	OO
3.	Throat	Blue	HA
4.	Heart	Green	YA
5.	Below the belly button	Yellow	RA

6. Genitals   Orange   VA

7. Base of the spine   Red   LA

These are the basic energy centers and their location and sound. Many people have used this chart, sometimes with a few variations of colors or sounds. I feel that these work best for me. Let us check how our connections are working in us right at this moment. I can almost feel mine move. You may desire to see them move for yourself. I can show you a way to do that.

You need to go to a novelty store or spiritual bookstore in your area. Buy a small pendulum with a cord or a long metal leash attached to it, one that seems to call to your spirit within. What it looks like does not matter for this test. When you have it at home and are ready to do your test, start by finding a room where you can lay down and feel comfortable. The less clothing you have, the better you will see the movement. Someone else can help you, or you can be all alone if needed.

Let us start with an easy one to begin with the Heart. It is the most powerful, and you can truly see how the pendulum will move. Take it in your right hand, or anyone else who is helping you do this can do that. Let the end of the pendulum drop down from the cord with the main weight at the bottom. Start just above the belly button at maybe 1 to 2 inches above your body. Slowly move up the middle of your body and watch what happens. If you move it slowly enough the energy field of the heart's outer edge will be located. It will tilt the bottom of the pendulum back a little toward to stomach. You can keep moving it forward to just above your heart.

It will do one of four things there. The most common is it will rotate in a circle. If it rotates clockwise, that is feminine and counter clockwise is male. Do not think of your gender. It is showing you how your heart is balanced. When I did my tests, mine was not in rotation. It moved from my head to my toes back and forth. That makes me more neutral. My energy centers are spinning in a turned position, which is not as common. There is one more that I have never seen but have heard about. It moves side to side and has also turned inside. You can check all your centers one by one and see them move. All should move a little like your heart but not as easily.

That is easiest way to test the energy centers. Once you get really good at it you may not need the pendulum. Know yourself and how your energy moves. If you do this practice, you will know how large your energy centers are and even how fast they may move. Later I will discuss how to change or move them for different kinds of energy work within.

More Energy Connections

Once you know how your energy moves within you, you will want to balance your energy centers fully and clean out any energies that may hinder their movement. I have found that breath energy is the best at doing this. It is easy to do alone or with others. Find a place where you can be calm, and you feel good about going inside yourself. Go to that spot and relax. Think of each of the energy centers on your body. You can picture them with color and how they are spinning on you.

Start at the bottom energy center. Look at a chart or remember where they are on your body. Focus on one center and visualize it moving. All the energy centers should be moving the same direction. Now I want you to take three deep breaths. Once you are done with that energy center go up to the next center right above that one. Breathe three deep breaths. Keep doing this all through all seven of the energy centers. Once you are done, you should feel energized. If you feel sick or dizzy, you may have other issues in one or more of the centers. Retest each one and find the one or a few that may need adjustment. I will show how to do the adjustments.

Energy Adjustments

Find the energy center or centers that need adjustment. Look at how they are moving. Are they spinning in the right direction or clogged by other outside energies? Are they all spinning in the same direction?

You may find an energy center that is clogged. If so, find a place again where you can relax and feel comfortable. Focus on that specific energy center. Visualize it moving, and put your right hand over the top of it. It should be spinning just below your hand. Visualize your hand reaching inside of it and grabbing on to the negative energy. Pull it slowly out and give it back to the universe. Do this at least three times. You can do this on all the energy centers that you feel need to be adjusted. Once you have done that and feel cleansed, you need to go back to breathing through all the centers again.

You may find an energy center spinning the wrong direction. If so, find a place you feel comfortable and relaxed. Focus on that one energy center. Visualize it moving in the wrong direction. Take your right hand and put it over the top of it. This time you want to slow the energy center down and stop it from spinning. This is not easy as clearing a clog. You must focus and visualize yourself reaching deep inside. As soon as you can, once you have it stopped, turn your hand within to start it spinning in the correct direction. You may need to do it more than three times. Keep doing it over and over until it stays flowing in the direction you wish it to go. Do this on all of the energy centers that need adjustment. When you have completed this adjustment, you need to go back and doing the breathing process again.

These are the basic ways to adjust the seven energy centers on the body. You have emotional energy deep within you and you may want to deep clean all the centers.

Healing Energy Adjustments

The ritual of healing is very sacred and must not be misused. It is a way to take out clogs or add something into an energy center. This takes a little more knowledge and understanding of how things work within the spiritual human body. The energy centers are set up just like our universe. All of them have a flow and pattern. Your heart center is the one that is the center and basis of all within your spirit. Everything always starts or finishes there. Most people balance themselves or the centers top to bottom or bottom to the top in a linear fashion. When you adjust them with knowledge and understanding of the true nature, you should do it clockwise or counter clockwise. "Shamans" for centuries have been doing this kind of healing.

Perhaps you are a woman and have an issue, any kind of issue. It is not the issue you deal with, but the spiritual energy of natural movement within that you adjust. The flow of energy in vibration connects them like a flow of water to go the way nature intended. All healing comes from the creative source of all living. You have that within you.

Consider your heart and how powerful it is. Your human body and spiritual being are connected to the entire universe. We all live in a plasma universe of connection. When you balance the energy of self and do it to the universes, all is healed. I have done this many times and know it works.

This is how it is done. Find a place of peace, calm and comfort. Sit or lie down and relax. Start at the heart. Focus on the energy breath of the heart connecting to the universe. Take three deep breaths and focus on the connection, feeling the energy of the universe breathing within you, becoming one, the same breath. Once this is established, you will know. You are in sync and one with all that lives. You are now connected in a powerful way. Take three deep breaths and let the universe know your intent of healing. You have three energy centers below the heart and three above. Balancing can begin on the other ones now.

Begin in a counter clockwise direction, going from the heart to the one just below or the one just above. It makes a difference which one you choose. At the energy centers, you must know if you wish to end at the top of your head or the base of your spine. If you start with the one below you will end at the top of the head. If you start at the one above the heart, you will end at the base of the spine.

Let us say you pick the one just below the heart, the fifth one down from the top. Focus now on that energy center. Take in the universe and feel its flow and vibration. You breathe in as one movement and energy. Take as many breaths as needed to feel oneness. You can put your hand or hands close by the center if needed. Use them to pull out any clogs or unwanted energy. Do this until you are totally balanced. Then move to the next center which is the third one from the top. Remember you are moving in a counter clockwise direction. Think of a circular motion. You went from the heart to just above the belly button and now you are at the throat. You are spinning with the universe and yourself. Do the same thing on this energy center. Focus on being one in flow and energy movement, breathing and pulling out any toxins.

Next will be the sixth center from the top at the genitals. Do the same again. Get balanced with the universe through breath and vibration. Get that center to become one, and pull out any unwanted energy. Now move on to the second center from the top. It is at the third eye, on your forehead. Balance that center to the universe, and make that energy one. Pull out all clogs or toxins. Do this as long as it takes until its energy is in the flow of the universe. Move to the energy center at the base of the spine, the seventh one from the top. You are now at the bottom of the centers. Breathe and focus its flow, as you clear out any toxins. Become one with the universe. Then it is on to the last and final energy center, at the top of the head or crown. Here is where place your focus and breathe. Feel its movement and balance it with the universe. Link your crown and head to all living beings. Feel the energy flow through the heart in a circle all the way out of the top of your head. It is so powerful, and now you are totally connected with all. You are healed.

Personal Energy Connections

Now we know how to basically connect energy by breathing through the centers. We have balanced ourselves, and there are no clogs or unwanted energy within. We can now connect deeply to others. This is my favorite part of connection. Two or more people can truly connect in a powerful union of oneness. You can share energy with others. This sharing of energy is life changing as you connect so deeply with another person. It can be done at a distance or right next to each other. Here are some examples of both.

I was online a number of years ago and chatting with a woman in San Francisco. I was living in San Diego. She was very spiritual, and we were talking about the energy centers on the body. I was telling her I was teaching breathing through the chakras and she wanted to learn how to do that. We both said it might be fun to set up a ritual where we could do the same movements at the same moment together. She liked the idea of trying it at a distance and seeing what it would do.

So we both set a time and place to do this together. We decided to sit on our beds at 9:00 pm and had our cell phones in speaker mode. We were talking, doing everything at the same time, both of us sitting comfortably and were naked. We had decided to have no restrictions that could disturb what we were trying to do. Just one soul to another in balance breathing through the energy centers and setting the tone using a Tibetan bowl, making a tone of three rings.

We felt very peaceful inside. I began by walking her through how to breathe through each of the chakras and on the third one how to make the sound related to it. We did each breathing set together and made the same sound at the same time. When we were done, we sat and felt each other within. I will admit this was so powerful for both us. We discovered that the distance makes no difference. We were connected and were wondering why others did not know about making this kind of connection. Over the years I have been working on the ritual and the method to get a better connection. My new friend enjoyed the connection so much she started teaching it in San Francisco the next week. Within a month she was teaching 10-20 students a month. It changed her life and mine too.

Another example involved meeting a young woman who wanted to learn my newfound method to connect in a powerful way. She was also spiritual. She wanted to do what I had previously done at a distance close up and personal. So we set up a place and time to do the same ritual face to face. We did the same three rings on the bowl and faced each other naked, though we were not being sexual. We only wanted to see how we could connect on a deep spiritual level. We started our breathing and went through all of the energy centers one by one, bottom to top. On the third breath made the sound related to it. This direct energy exchange was even more powerful than the one I had done at a distance. We felt oneness to each other and to life. It changed the both of us as we now understood how to truly connect with others. Many years have passed since these experiences happened at a distance and close up, so I know people can connect doing breathing with intent.

The Tantric Connection

Years later, I was talking with a woman about what one could do with breathing and connection. She said that it sounded very much like "Tantric Breathing". I was surprised as I always thought Tantra was a sexual experience. She said that some of it is, and the part I had been teaching was the other part of it, since it was about connection too. So I started to read all I could on the Tantra connection. She was right about it as I discovered that for thousands of years people have been doing the connecting I have been teaching. Wow! That was validation enough for me. I now have this knowledge and use it in my rituals and teachings to help people connect more deeply within themselves and with others.

If you make the energy breathing connection and are intimate sexually at the same time, you'll experience "True Bliss". I will not get into all the details here. Let us just say that you are joined sexually in a position called the "Yaba Yum". Doing the breathing and connection ritual as one is beyond belief. You will experience great joy as you do the intimate breathing, kissing and caring in a face-to-face connection. If married people and those in love do this kind of connecting, they will find great happiness in their relationship. It is the only kind of loving relationship my being can accept and will do. This is what I believe in.

A Tantric connection is of being one with all and desiring joy and love in life. Learn more about this kind of connection to see if you desire it too. Go to your bookstore and read about Tantric connecting. I did and it changed my thoughts on intimate connections. The best book I found is *The Idiot's Guide to Tantra*. I loved it and found many of the things I talk about concerning connections. Do not let the title fool you or make you feel like you are an idiot. It is just a brand name used to catch the reader's attention and get sales.

Relationships

We have many relationships in our lifetimes including:

1. Family
2. Friends
3. Lovers
4. Co-workers and bosses
5. Community
6. Nation
7. Planet
8. Universe
9. God or Creator

We must ask ourselves how each of these is personal to us. Do our emotions influence our thinking? The answer is yes. They do affect us all deeply!

My emotions are very deep and strong. I have shed many tears over the years though I have not shown them. I feel I must stay in control of my emotions. I get really quiet when I get emotional. I want to cry in front of others, but I just cannot do it. I do not want to show weakness in being a man. To many people that makes me misunderstood, and some think I do not care. Yet, I do care very deeply. I was brought up by loving parents that had different thoughts on how a man should act. Women could cry but not men.

I was a young boy of five or six, I cried almost every day for two years. My skin had big boils about the size of half dollars. Once a week my doctor would give me penicillin shots to get rid of the infections in my body. My mother used to sit with me and pop each one of them with a needle. She would push out the pus on all sides of each one. It was so painful. It would happen every night for two to three hours. This was not fun for me or my family as it did affect everyone. Finally, after the boils went away, my parents decided there would be no more crying from me. I was to learn to be a man and was yelled at as I was being told not to cry anymore. Many years later my mother said she was sorry for that. She wished I was okay with showing my emotions. However, my parents had done a really good job of teaching me how to hold them in. Even as I am writing this, I have strong feelings about that time and I know I hold them deep inside.

Many years have passed. My mother passed on at 55. She was too young to die. She had breast and lung cancer. And I did not cry! Fitting I guess, yet so sad. I had turned into the man who cannot cry, even for my beloved mother. I really miss her. Smoking killed her and took her from my life. She was my best friend; we used to talk about everything. So many years later now, it is still hard to think of her as gone. Though I know she is doing well and in a great place, as I have visited her many times in the mansion worlds. I will be very happy when it is my turn to leave this world, so I can see her again and give her a big hug and a soft kiss. She was the best and I was very glad she was my mother. I will always remember her saying to me, "Be open and honest. Do not judge yourself or others. Listen to others and be their friend. Be free, be happy and enjoy life. All the good and the bad are part of life. I love you and always will." She was always there for me. That is what is on her grave stone: "Always There".

How fitting that my relationships have evolved over the years as I come to understand who I am. As I learn how to deal with the world around me, I am cautious and reserved, yet I am opening up over time and I want to truly show myself to others. Most of time, I have been misunderstood and words simply do not explain who I am. This writing has become the most I have ever have opened up to show the world the real me. As you read my words, I am hoping I will be understood as the loving, caring man I am. I thank you for being part of my life.

Manifesting

Life is one of manifesting desires into reality. How does that happen? You think about something and it manifests. However, it is not always a sure thing. You need to keep thinking about something long enough and keep feeling it deep inside, until it starts to grow. Your body will start to gravitate toward people who can and will get you that result. What if there is something you need to have in your life? Is there a ritual you can do to get a result? Yes there is. This is what I found works.

You need to find a place where you can get comfortable in your surroundings. Set up a space of time when you will not be disturbed. Make this a sacred space or room in that moment. You can do that by doing a few things. If you have sage or candles use them to clear the space. Light the sage or candle and walk around the room. In every corner or at every window ask the creator of all to bring good energy into the room and take all bad stuck energy out. Once you have done this, set a tone of energy within the room. Some people use a drum or a Tibetan singing bowl. Tap the drum or bowl three times to set the tone.

The next thing you need to do is clear your energy centers. Do this by breathing through each center three times, and use the sound that goes with that center on your last breath. You can use the chart in this book or another one you feel drawn to. The one here always seems to work well for me.

Once you have your energy centers ready and clear, begin to build the energy around you. You can sit or lie down. Relax and feel the energy around your body. If you are sitting, get comfortable and have your hands on your knees with the palms of your hands facing up. Your fingers should be open and upward too. If you are lying down, your hands should be by your sides. Your arms should go down toward your feet with the palms up and fingers upward. When you do either of these positions, you need to just feel the energy around you. Feel how it moves. Start to visualize the energy and its power. In your hands feel the warmth of the energy.

Now take the energy you feel in your hands and visualize it growing into balls of energy just above each hand. The ball is about 8 to 10 inches in size. Feel it spin in your hands as it glows brightly. Think of the energy in your right hand as male energy and in the left hand as female. Let them grow and pulse brightly. Do this for a few minutes and feel how they move. Ask the creator of all life to listen to the energy that is created in your hands. You can do this in your mind or say this out loud. I like to be vocal as it seems to work better and feels strong within me. Thank the creator of all for your life and say anything else you wish to say.

Take the two energy balls in your hands and put them together as one big ball of light. The ball should be about 18 to 25 inches round now. Feel the energy of the sphere in your hands. Say in a loud voice what you wish to manifest. "I want to bring into my life…". You need to do this at least three times. Let your thoughts and desire go into the energy ball in your hands. See it grow and turn brighter. Feel its energy and the glow it gives the whole room.

The next thing you need to do is release the ball of energy into the universe. Lift it up and push it out of your hands. Say, "I give my energy, thoughts and desires to the universe so they will manifest in my life." Do this with joy in your heart and with the love you have for yourself and all of creation. This can be an emotional experience. I hope it is for you. When you have emotion in your heart and soul, the real intent is much stronger. You may cry and that is okay and part of the release of energy you have to give.

Relax and enjoy what has happened to you in this moment. You and the universe are one. Enjoy the feeling. You may want to rest or sleep, or you may have been filled with energy and want to be active. All are good. It is a great feeling. The universe knows what you want and need now in your life. Have peace of mind that it will happen, and never doubt. When you do this exercise, your manifestation can happen at any moment. Be ready and open to receive it, as that is just as important as releasing it to the universe.

Future Manifesting

The future is the manifestation of our thoughts at present. We bring the future to us with each thought. Our desire to have a certain future makes it become our present. We manifest it and make it real. We do it every day of our lives and most people do not even care how it happens. What if we did it with a focus? We can and it works. You think it, say it and do it with intent. Be true to your real desire and it happens. If you want happiness, money or a better job, all can be manifested. Do not think of bad things or they will come too, just as easily. You make your future; no one else does it for you.

Each morning think about your real intent and desires. What do you want? What do you need? What kind of experience do you want in life? Then do the manifesting practice and watch miracles unfold in your life.

Protection Grid

Many people have asked me about those who use manifesting to attack others or to call on the dark side of energy. There is no real dark side. There can be people or groups of people who have their own agenda and use energy that might not be good for you. It is not usually to attack you directly, but it can happen. I have found a way to protect myself and to block out unwanted energy around me. I teach how to do this and will show you how. By creating an energy field, you can be in the right place, in the right moment for your protection.

All of what I do is about the flow of energy and how to use it wisely. The first thing you need to do is set a time and a place to do the ritual of building a protection grid or sphere. I want you to get a personal natural item. A stone or crystal will do. It must be something you can carry with you all the time. The first time I did this ritual, I went to a store that had beryl stones. These stones have a unique pattern within them, and I was really drawn to the pattern. It just felt right for me. You can pick some object you feel really good about. Once you have that stone or object, get ready to do the ritual.

You have the place and time set. The mood in the room should be peaceful and calm. You can again set the mood by ringing a Tibetan bowl three times. If you do not have one it is okay. There is no right or wrong way to set the mood, just have your intent. You can play soft music or burn incense. Candles are also a nice way to get comfortable. All of these items are to get you feeling peaceful and good inside.

Once the mood is set, you are ready to get started. Clear out all your energy centers with the breathing ritual or whatever may work for you. Set the personal item you have in front of you as it will be part of the ritual. Now that all your energy centers are open and clear it is time to begin. I want you to sit or lay down if it is easier. Put your hands out in front of you, and place your hands with the palms turned upward. Your arms can rest on your knees. If you are lying down, face your hands toward your feet and the palms up.

In your mind visualize energy coming to you and resting in both of your hands. It is like a ball or sphere of energy, 8-10 inches in diameter and spinning. The right hand is male energy and the left is female. Focus on the flow, and feel it energy in your hands, bright and glowing. Thank the energy for being present with you. Tell the energy and the universe you wish to use this energy to protect you from harm and be a shield for your spirit. Tell the energy and the universe that the stone or item in front of you is the key and the grounding point of the grid that will be around you. You will keep it with you always or close by.

Ask the energy in both hands to send energy to the item or stone. Notice the energy is now forming a triangle. This is the start of the grid and the pattern that will go over you.

Ultimately, it will look like a circle with triangular shapes that are linked together. Next take both energy balls in your hands and put them together into one bigger ball around 16 to 25 inches. Feel the energy as it forms and watch how brightly it glows. Say to the energy and the universe that you want it to grow and become so large it covers you and at least 3 or 4 feet around you. Let it grow and do just that. Once that is done feel the energy again as it surrounds your whole body now. Ask the energy and the key to set the grid or matrix pattern. It will do this,and you will now have the total shield of protection. Thank the energy and the universe for their help. You have a key that should stay with you always or within the same room.

I put my beryl stone on a pendant with a chain that I wear around my neck. It worked so well for me, and it was beautiful. I am sure you can think of different ways to hold yours.

Myth and Belief

I was helping a friend do her energy balancing, when she stopped me and said, "I don't understand what kind of readings you are getting with the pendulum and testing." I was feeling that she was very well balanced and flowing in spirit daily. I said, "You are balanced; the flow is really good." She asked, "Then why is my energy going from my head to my toes, up and down? Does that not mean I'm blocked?" I looked at her and understood that she was confused.

I told her, "You have been told that your energy should be moving in a clockwise motion. Most people believe in the energy centers and think they're like a disc. I'm going to tell you the truth. They're like a ball of light, and not disc shaped. The truth is that each one is like the natural laws of nature. The universe and our bodies are set up in the same way. We have energy fields within. That is the flow and energy we see when we test the chakras or energy centers with a pendulum or our hands. Many people over the years test or interpret it incorrectly. They were trained or they learned incorrectly how they work. They did not learn from spirit the full understanding of the universe. Your flow is correct and flowing through your body and it is good."

The flow of energy through all the energy centers can be flowing in any direction. Just a full balancing of the fields to the same flow is needed. In the example above, she was flowing from top to bottom and vice versa. She was free flowing and balanced. If all your centers are flowing clockwise, that is good too. It is free flowing. The same can be said about them moving counter clockwise. That is just as good. The fields change and flip just like our solar system and the universe. Everything has cycles. There are no blockages with free flowing through the energy centers. Now if one of the centers is flowing in a different direction from the others, there needs to be an adjustment. Here are some things to do when this happens.

If your heart moves counter clockwise and the other centers are moving clockwise, you need to ask yourself what changes are happening to you with love or deep emotional feelings. Look deep within yourself. The heart is the main center for all your emotions. It beats with energy and sends it to all the other centers. All your centers will change following the heart. That means change is within you and your desires. Each one of the energy centers has a purpose and a separate field of energy. When all the fields flow the same way, all is good. If any of them are turning in a different direction than the others, you need to go within for the reason.

Maybe the first one at the base of the spine is off or spinning differently than the others. Look at some possible reasons. The first chakra is a grounding or a root to this planet's energy field. Ask yourself if you feel grounded. Do you ever go barefooted? Do you go to nature and see the wilderness? Do you feel one with the earth? Those are some things that might cause the imbalance. Look at your connection to this planet.

Maybe the second one at the genitals is spinning differently. Ask yourself about your physical being. Do you take care of your body like a temple? Is your energy slow, or do you feel tired all the time? How is your sex life? All these are good questions to ask yourself. Make a change that will balance this center. The 3rd energy center, listen to what your gut tells you. Are you stressed about what is going on in your life? Do you eat the wrong foods? Do you have difficulty relaxing or enjoying life? Look inside and make a change. Meditate more and find calm in connection with yourself and others.

The heart is the most powerful energy center. It really does have a cause and effect in your life in so many ways. I could write a book just on this energy center and still not fully explain how important it is. It is literally the bloodline to all that is physical and spiritual. Ask yourself what are you connected to in life. What are your desires? Are you choosing the right things for yourself? This energy center needs to be your main focus. Get this one right and all the others will follow.

The energy center at the neck is a focus of how you relate to others. Ask yourself if you listen or hear what others say. Do you speak words without any real meaning? Do you feel misunderstood? Change how you relate to others. Look at why people see you like they do. Look inside and see yourself.

The energy center at the third eye is the one that sees the unknown. Ask yourself if you are you open to new thoughts. Are there too many things in your life and you have trouble staying focused? Free your mind of all that is blocking you to grow. Change your thoughts within.

The last energy center at the top of your head is the opening to all around you. Ask yourself how you feel about God. How do you feel about the universe? Do you feel connected? Open the door inside. Think about changing your life and thinking of new ideas. Be creative and become one.

Section III

Personal Experiences

My Personal Change

Personal change is always constant. Everything in the known and the unknown is always in constant flux. I know I am here now and forever will be. When my body becomes dust, my spirit remains. My spirit also lives on in others whom my life has touched. They are with me too. Life is a gift so use it well. It will serve you in the next part of your journey. I think of all the people I have met past, present and future, and I know I will always be your friend. Life is very short, and it is like a blink of an eye to the thought of forever. It is now you see it, and now you don't. Memories fill lifetimes of learning. I look forward to seeing you in this life and the next. We shall embrace and rejoice together.

I had a vision the other night. I was not frightened or scared. You cannot force things to be a certain way. If it was meant to be, there is no way of stopping it. I see my death or change of spirit coming. It will come for me, and someday it will come for you. I am ready and embrace its coming.

Whitecloud

Many people have asked me about my name. I received it about 20 years ago. In all my travels to different realms and other worlds, my given name did not seem to be right for me. So I asked my guide and the creative spirit to give me a new name, one I could use in this and the other worlds. They told me I could do a ritual and get my new name. Here it is.

Prepare yourself to have some alone time. Go to your special place where you can relax and have a mirror with you. Once you feel in tune within yourself, look in the mirror. If you do not have mirror then imagine you are standing in front of yourself. Look deeply at yourself and see into your soul. Picture a ball of light at your heart and see it glow. You are a spiritual being and your brightness shines.

Say into the mirror, looking at your spirit three times each:

1. "I request to know my new name."
2. "Hear me my guides and creator of all that is."
3. "Let me hear, see and understand."
4. "Give me the light energy sound."
5. "Tell me my new name."

After saying these three times each, find a private place to listen for answers. It works best if you are by running water or still water. It can be a pond, river, pool or bath tub. Be calm and start listening to all that is around you. Feel the energy and its flow. You will hear in a soft voice saying your new name. It will be wonderful. Then say it and confirm you received it. It is now yours. You now have an authentic name.

Mine is Dane Whitecloud. I heard it as a full name. You may only hear one word for your name, not a first and last name. Here is something to think about. This name was given to you and can be just for you only. It can be for your spirit in the spirit worlds or for your guides. Maybe even for some of your close family members. Feel its energy in you when you say it. I have taught many others to do this and it really does work. I hope you try it and are happy with your new name.

Most people will not understand why people should do this. It is a personal thing to do. It is a connection to yourself and all that is spiritual. You may be tempted to tell everyone about this, so I advise you to be calm and check your feelings. Tell only those who are worthy of your spirit, and when it feels right inside. Your guides and spirits you will see on your travels will call you by that name from now on. You are connected to it. Enjoy life and take a deep breath. Remember who you are within.

Choices

A new day is here. I wake up most days very early and even see the sun rise in the east. My spirit is in a change mode again. It seems like every seven to 10 years this happens. Everything I see and do for the next year will be looked at inside and out—my work, spiritual thoughts and even who will be around or who my being is attracted to. It is all choices from within.

Should I turn right or left, or maybe even do nothing. All these choices are never right or wrong, but they are made every day. We need to focus and take a deep breath before each choice. Learning to breathe deep breaths of energy, help you choose the best path. Always look at things openly, honestly and with passion. There are many deep questions of who, what and where our life is going. My life experience and my connections are unfolding, as are yours. Change and choices are beautiful things. What will they be? Am I ready? Are you ready?

A Connection of Life

Breath is the connection to all of life. It is the key that opens the door to inner changes of spirit and light vibration. Breath is the energy exchange with all life. With every breath we take, we exchange the energies of light and sound. We do this daily and in a sharing way. When you focus this energy in and out of the energy centers of the body, the universe unfolds within you. We are all one and connected through sharing our breath with all of life.

Point of View

Stop and listen to the sounds within. Can you hear the high pitch ringing in your ears? It is the energy sound current of life.

^^^^^^^^^^^^^^^^^^^^^^CURRENT^^^^^^^^^^^^^^^^^^^^^^

It is everywhere we go, and is the movement of life all around us. Some of us hear nothing, just the regular sounds of nothing. Yet many people hear the sound. Close your eyes and listen. Can you hear it within? Focus on your point of view. It is yours and yours alone.

We feel in many ways in this life experience. You feel with touch. You feel with emotion. You even feel for understanding. What is hot or cold? What is up or down? What is happy or sad? The understanding of it is limited. We all see, hear and feel, then take the point of view we understand. Do we understand now or thousand years from now? Do we judge what we understand? Can you let it be? Can you change what is? The answer is yes we can do all of the above. We do it every mini-second of our lives.

Thoughts pass through our minds instantly as we receive them. We sort and place them into an order that makes sense to us. Thoughts are never discarded just refilled. Some are never used, and others we use all the time. We are a mass storage unit of answers and choices. The mind stores it all. Whatever you have ever thought or done is there. What we do with this information is a whole different process altogether.

Many teachers of thought have said to take these actions: "Clear your mind," "Embrace yourself" or "Focus". All of them work in limitation. Ask yourself what you believe. Do you believe everything you hear, see or feel? What exactly do you believe in? The answer is that whatever you believe is your reality. It is your point of view. It is how you look at the world and make sense of it.

This is what I believe:

1. Belief is a flow of thought.
2. It is a process of updating.
3. It is a renewal of each moment of reality.
4. It changes my ideas and my belief of what is.
5. I am "thought in process" constantly.

There is a time to clear your mind, embrace yourself or just focus. It fits with my belief and thoughts. These thoughts are like food and are always feeding us in what we see, hear and feel. I love to eat and so do you.

Thoughts

I have said earlier in this book, that if you have thought it you have done it. So let us move on to the next thought. We do this all of the time: we think thought to thought to thought. The flow of thoughts passes through different parts of the brain and is processed. Beware of thoughts not processed, which blocks the flow within. It looks like this. One thought is stacked upon another.

Thought
Thought
THOUGHT

The thoughts that build up within you turn into physical manifestations. They can become a mountain and take over your life. You say to yourself, "I just need to do this kind of thing. If I can just get this done I will be fine." This builds that mountain of thoughts. You can avoid them, dive into them or look at them piece by piece. All are choices you have. Thoughts are not really avoidable, but you can believe you have avoided them. You can dive into a thought and stay focused on that thought only. If you do this, you will look inside, and after a while you will question the process. Lastly, you can look at a thought piece by piece. If it sounds like a good idea, then follow up on it. You may have thoughts of where to begin when you follow each thought.

The present moment is your reality, and now is about thoughts. Change occurs from second to second, and even faster than that. If you think a mountain is a mountain, then it really is. If you can think it gone, it is. Gone! No stagnant thought. Move on. There is no past, no future, just the now thought. We need to live in the now. That is the answer.

Fluid Thoughts

I really enjoy talking with others and feeling the flow of fluid thought. The ideas pass through our heads and come right out of our mouths. When two people are in a spiritual flow of thought, they can discuss topics that are truly profound. Wow! It is great fun to do. It is uplifting, and sometimes even unexpectedly open in what you discuss. You ask questions and get answers. They are real answers to deep questions. Some of the answers can take years to fully understand. Yet, some of them you understand instantly. When you are in the flow of fluid thought with another spiritual person, it can last just a few minutes or many hours or days. You only have to be willing to be open to listening within and connecting with the other person or persons. The conditions around you must be calm and comfortable. I am always looking for others to take part in this kind of thought.

You can also have self fluid thought. That is often how writers write profound words. I have done that sometimes for this book. Words just flow out of my mind onto the paper. When that happens, it is cool to read later. You can say, "I wrote that so easily." It was inspirational flow of fluid thought, and it can happen at any time to anyone. It can last only a few minutes or hours. This book has been written off and on over many years. Many of its passages were through fluid thought, having only written when I was inspired or needed to write it down not to forget what happened.

My Past Lives

I have had many dreams and visions over the years. There are places in the mansion worlds and beyond that show you your past lives. You can visit them or see them on your travels within. I have had three of these kinds of visions. They are very vivid and full in scope. You can see a whole lifetime in a short vision, like it is compressed into your thought. I will tell you of my visions of my past lives I have seen through the veil.

In my first vision and dream of a past life, I was in the Roman times. I am not sure of the exact date. maybe about 400 BC. My name was Clavious, and I was a soldier in the Roman army. Life was very brutal and difficult. I killed men and children and raped women. I was the commander and part of a group of soldiers that lived in a region in the northern part of Rome, what some would say now is part of southern France. It was near the Po River. I was married, had kids, and two older brothers and two younger sisters.

In my job, I was in charge of about 80 to 200 men at a time. We guarded the river and controlled all the people there. The legion's clothes were black and we had very little armor. We took what we needed, and the people living near us served us in any way we desired, as if they were our slaves. If you did not do what we asked, you died or were maimed. We only cared about ourselves, and many suffered at my hands and those of my men. My death came by the sword when I was beheaded. Looking at this past life of hardship, pain and suffering, I learned so much. So much compassion is within my heart, as well as an understanding of loss and feeling for those who died at my hands. My life was a controlling life. Power and control of others is why I was there.

My second vision and dream of a past life was in the northern part of what we now call England. The time was around 700 AD. My name was Froje and I was a French man living in a village on the east coast on the British island. It was always wet. There were not any roads, mostly just ships coming in and going out. Maybe less than 100 people lived there with no families or friends. I worked with fish and was also a butcher of meats, lamb or pigs being my stock in trade. My hands were always bloody and smelled of death.

This was a time of despair for most people, not having much work. And plants did not grow very well either. Everyone was just trying to survive. I spoke many different languages, and that helped me fit in, though it made others hate me. I was beaten many times over the years. There was much sickness in the land with most people being sick or dying of some kind of illness. The suffering was great to all, and I never met one happy person in this lifetime. I died at a young age of sickness. Some of the people called it a plague or a curse from God. I learned so much from this experience too. My life was one of submission, with no power or control of anything.

In my third vision and dream of a past life, I was a woman in the Mayan Empire in North America, maybe 1000 AD, though I am not really sure. My name was Olma, and my village was dominated by men. Women were important to the men for sex and having babies. Women did play a role of helping the men and were a part of a group family. All children were their children. The women enjoyed helping other women. Again it was a life of survival. You had a place to eat and sleep. As a woman I had sex, childbirth at a young age and had two children. There were many fights between villages, and many people suffered. It was common to be raped often as it was part of life. Having children and being part of a group made life a little better. Death came soon in this life. I was still young and died during the birth of my third child, a son, who survived. This was a life of understanding of what it is to be a woman. Having no power and a little control, I learned compassion and sharing.

In my current life as a man, from my childhood until now, my life has been a roller coaster ride. My parents were good, but had their flaws as all people do. I was raised to have an open mind and to be respectful of others. My parents had me when they were 18. Both my mother and father were still in high school, and I was not planned. They decided to get married and keep me.

My dad went into the Air Force, and my mom became a stay-at-home mother. My dad did graduate from high school, though my mother did not until many years later. This was 1953, and the rules were strict on how it should be for families. You did not have children out of wedlock. I was born in Louisiana, and my sister was born in Germany two and half years later. I was a happy kid and really enjoyed getting into trouble. My mother had her hands full. I was always trying new things and learning how things worked. Drawing was my passion as a kid, and I loved to create pictures of stars, squares, circles and triangles. They all seemed to have meaning to me deep inside. Art and having fun were all I thought about as a child. It is so strange how much of life you remember. All the little things are just like it was yesterday.

I also hold memories of historical events for the world. The day President Kennedy was shot in Dallas, Texas. The moon landing in 1969. The 60s were a troubled time, as we wanted so much and change was happening everywhere. While life in the 50s was very ordered, and we had to conform, the 60s were the complete opposite. It was a time of freedom and not conforming. I was in high school and graduated in 1972. Nixon was our President, and people thought he was a crook. The war in Vietnam was on everyone's mind, and I was in the last draft for the military. However, I was not drafted, yet so many of my friends were. I went to college instead, seeking my place in the world, trying to live a life of happiness and love. My life as an adult began.

I have had many experiences, and I am sure you have too. Then seeing these past life visions opened up my mind to the idea of many lives and experiences. Looking into my past lives was fun. I may have had many more, but was only shown three. They are the ones I needed to know currently in this life. The records may show me having up to 57 lives, some from the last 10,000 years and others from the ancient past. I will look at them all if needed and desired. You can look at your own lives too. The choice is yours. You can find a medium or a person who can access the records, or you can go to the hall of records in the mansion worlds. Your guide can help you do that.

Near Death Experiences

This life has been one of making choices, and some of them have been for me to experience being close to death. Three times in my life I have been close to it, due mostly to getting into trouble as a boy. My mother was always worried what I would get into next, because of my wanting to have fun and experience things, not thinking or looking what I was doing. No doubt in my mind, the guides and angels around me were watching over me. Most of what happened to me had me inches or seconds from death.

My first near death experience (NDE) was when I was five years old. Riding my tricycle was my passion. When on my tricycle, life was always fun. I liked to go fast and feel the air go by me. My family lived in Pasadena, California in my grandmother's house. There were cool sidewalks to ride on with driveways that sloped down to the streets. This particular day was beautiful, and the skies were clear. It was about 10:00 a.m. I decided to go around the corner and see what was down the street. There were more homes and cool driveways. A few doors down was this very high driveway. Wow! I could go really fast down that one, so I went over and climbed up it with my bike.

At first going down, I used the pedals but it did not seem

fast enough. Going back up the drive again, this time using no pedals, I wanted to see how fast the tricycle could go, and it was very fast. I was going so fast that I went past the sidewalk over the curb and into the street. As I was coming out into street and having a great time, I looked in front of me and saw a car going by and I hit it on the side. The car was going about 25 miles an hour. My tricycle went under the tires in the back and fell off to the side, while my body was bounced off the side of the car. What a loud sound it made. The car stopped, and a man ran out and looked at me. He said, "I didn't even see you."

Standing right up and looking at him, I wondered where the car had come from. Not having a scratch or a bump on me, I noticed I was totally fine. My mother heard the sound, and she and all the people living in the area came out to look. If I had gone down that driveway two seconds earlier, I would have been in front of the car and not hit its side. Death can happen that quickly, and that day it did not happen to me. This has always made me feel guided and cared for.

The second time I was guided and watched over was when I was in the fifth grade, which was a good time for me. My parents had moved to Florida in 1965, and we lived in a town called Coco Beach. It is only a few miles south of Cape Canaveral where my father was working. He was a test engineer and was helping with the space program to put a man on the moon. Life was really fun there. We lived one block from the beach and one block from the river that moves around Coco Beach. I remember the first time I saw my first rocket blast off; it was a special moment for me.

It was our first day in Coco Beach. At 2:00 a.m., my parents woke my sister and me up. We walked down to the beach in the pitch black darkness in our slippers. We sat down in the sand and looked out at the water. It was cool but not cold. We sat for about five minutes, and then all of sudden there was a loud sound and right in front of us in the water there was this really bright light. A rocket was being shot out of a submarine in the ocean. Wow! It was incredible and I will always remember it. Now back to my near death experience.

My life in Florida was one of swimming, fishing and having fun all day long. One day, we were swimming at the Ramada Inn, a few blocks from our house, in their huge pool. I was always in the water doing something. They had a diving board there that was long and high, and it called me to do flips off of it into the pool. My mother and sister were there. Watching me doing a front flip and then a back flip too. I was always pushing my limits to go higher or turn a different way on the board. So this time, I jumped on the end of the board and pulled my feet over my head in a flip. As I came down, my face hit the diving board. It tore away half of my face from my nose to my chin. I had hit the end of the board and then hit the water.

I came up screaming. The water turned bright red, and everyone got out of the pool. I swam to the end where my mother pulled me out of the water. Many towels were put on my face, and then I was rushed to the hospital. I was in surgery for three hours and had over 400 stitches in my mouth. I had a brace on my face and could not even move my mouth or jaw. I was wheeled out of surgery in a wheel chair. My mother saw me and passed out; it took a few minutes for her to recover. I went home the same day wearing a brace, which I had on for two months. I had to eat through a straw for over a month and could not laugh. It hurt so bad to even move my lips. They said I was lucky, and that if it was one inch over, I would have hit my nose bone head on, and it would have gone right into my brain killing me instantly. I felt I had made another choice to do something with my guides and angels watching me again. How close is less than one inch to death?

My third experience was in 1972 when I was a senior at Azusa High School in Azusa California. My best friend Stephan and I were always doing something together. We used to sing songs and play guitar. We played basketball almost every day, because he was the star player on the high school team. He was 6'6" and since I was only 5'10", I played on the tennis team.

We decided to skip school on a Friday morning and go on an adventure in his new car. He had a very cool suped up Ford Maverick. The weather was nice and the skies were blue, with the mountains off in the distance having snow on them. They called to us to go see them. It was about a half hour to the bottom of the mountains and the main road to get there. Stephan was driving and I was sitting watching the side of the road as we hit a section where the road went up and down like a roller coaster. We both enjoyed how it felt in his new car, so he stopped and turned around. We wanted to feel that again, this time going much faster. We were almost at 60 miles an hour, and we left the ground, just like in the "Dukes of Hazard". Wow! Then when we hit the ground, we were no longer on the road and were eight to 10 feet off the road on the dirt next to the road. There were four steel poles in front of us and a metal shack. We went right through the middle of them missing them by only a few feet. We were still going at least 50 miles an hour.

The car started to turn, and both of us were yelling, "Oh shit". Going another 100 feet, the nose of the car went into a ditch as the back of the car flipped over the front and we came to a stop upside down. My friend went out half way through his open window, and I was curled up into a ball, thrown to the roof of the car and into back seat area. We were not wearing seat belts. In 1972 you did not have to wear them. Five or 10 minutes passed, and then I woke up from a daze, crawled out my side of the car, stood up and felt fine. Not a scratch or any broken bones. Walking slowly around the car, I saw Stephan lying there. He was moaning and said he felt pain. I walked to the road to flag down a car to get help. A few people driving by saw our car and stopped. The police and an ambulance came to take my friend to the hospital. I was taken there too. Nothing happened to me at all, but I did have a feeling of tightness in the back of my neck. It remains tight even today.

My friend was not as lucky. He broke his neck in two places and was in traction for over a year. He never played basketball again, and as for me, I lost my best friend that day because his parents never wanted me to see him again. Many years later, I ran into him and asked him to forgive me for ditching school that day. He did not reply, and I never saw him again. My guides were there again, I am sure of it. The many obstacles we missed at 50 miles an hour would have killed us. The poles or the shack were only 10 feet apart. I have been to the spot many times over the years, and it is still hard to believe we missed them. So close to death again and yet I am still alive. I must still have much to do with my life.

I went back to school that year and played on the tennis team, and we won a league championship. Funny, I did plan to tell my parents what had happened that day, but my life at that time had changed. My parents had just gotten a divorce and life was not so good. They never knew about this accident. I then moved out on my own and never lived with my parents again.

These experiences have shown me a different view of how our guides and angels around us help us out. They do not tell us you cannot do something. They let you make your own mistakes. They are here to assist you and comfort you with issues sometimes beyond your control. They do seem to help, at least in my case, in keeping me from harm, though I am not sure if that is how they work for everyone. It makes me wonder how many close calls each person has in their lifetime. Maybe we have had a few more and do not even realize we were being helped. You may have some yourself, a close call or near death experience. It may be part of the human experience. It is nice know that having my inner guide always around does help me to be more careful.

I Am Dane Whitecloud

I am Dane Whitecloud. The years have now passed, and all who know me now call me Dane. The only time my given name is used is on anything legal. As a teacher and a student of life, the energy of my inner being shows me what to explore. My desire is to enjoy life and teach others simple rituals and habits to help make their lives better. I bring a little bit of the old and a little of the new. This helps keep the mind calm and safe. A rush to change everything a person knows can confuse someone who believes a certain way about how things are. I prefer to teach those who are ready for what I have to present. Many are searching for something new, yet only a few will understand and are ready for the change. If you are reading this and have gotten this far, you may be one of those who are ready.

Being a creative being is what my life is for. To be creative with the one source of creation gives me energy. Teaching others is my creative outlet to help and care for people. I want them to learn something they can use for a lifetime. Who will I teach? Where will I teach? When or even why I will teach them? My experiences have brought me to this point in my life. How will I share what I know to be true inside? Many need to know how to do meditation, healing, looking within, rituals, traveling

131

in spirit, art, music of the soul or they just need a muse to help them understand themselves. Again, I just want to help in any way I can. Ask and I will try to help if needed. That is my goal and purpose currently on this planet.

Having had many jobs over the span of my life, what some would call "a Jack of all trades", I have learned so much. And I know some of it has been the wrong stuff. Yet, I learned how to deal with others and having made a lot of money over the years. Sometimes though, I had not even enough to get by. Every dollar takes a toll and a price on what you will accept in life. Life is a school of learning to understand who you are inside. Some people only look outside at what they do in life. Their life is about cars, homes and keeping an image for their friends. If you do not go within in this life, you will be back in another life until you do. It is about choices and listening to that voice within, asking yourself: Is there more to this life than this?

More Thoughts and Memories

My memories keep flowing through me and I want to write them down. As I have said, my childhood was one full of mischief and being curious, always getting into trouble. My mother had her hands full. I enjoyed teasing my sister and having fun. Running naked or just seeing how fast my body could run was great. I did not like to fight or get hurt, and no conflict was my thought; I would rather run away than punch anyone. Much of my life has always been sensual or sexual, even at an early age when I enjoyed being playful. It was never a thought of right or wrong; I loved kissing girls, and it felt good and I liked it.

When I became an adult, that interest did not go away. Maybe it was their smell or soft skin that made me be playful. In my whole life I have been obsessive with the women around me. Everything about them I enjoyed and loved. They are truly amazing creatures. To this day, though, I do not understand why they do what they do, how they think or why they feel so much. I really honor them and respect who they are. They are a gift to men in every way. It bothers me when men disrespect them or abuse them in any way. Women should be in charge of their own lives. They should have all the choices of what happens in everything they do. Their choices of who they love is for each woman to decide. Men are not their rulers telling them how to live and love.

My life is a full one, having known a few women over the years. I love to see women in love. They have so much hope inside of the future. They feel joy their lives when they are loved. I too enjoy being in love. It could be a soft kiss, a warm heart of caring. When two people are in love and the feeling is deep inside, they are open to sharing their hopes and dreams together. It is like heaven is putting its arms around them. It would be nice if it was like that all the time. But, as we all know that is not the case. It happens rarely, thought it does happen for some. Yet others never know it at all and wish they could experience it. Total unconditional love that is shared and becoming one is what I want. I wish that for all who live in this world.

Communication and Forgiveness

The trials of life each day take a toll on everyone. We all have had so many different life experiences. To maintain our sanity and our relationships, communication is the key. In my life, I have not done that very well. I always thought I was good at communication, but now, looking back at my relationships, I know that is not true. People misunderstand me and who I really am, having not been very clear in my thoughts or actions over the years. My words are not clearly understood, so it is a flaw I have learned to deal with and work to overcome. I try to improve my communication each day, and I think I am getting better at it. People only see what they think I am. I deeply want everyone to see me as a really caring, loving soul, as that is what I am now.

I wish to say to the world, "If I have ever offended anyone or hurt them in any way, I am sorry. Please forgive me. Understand I am just a man with flaws, feeling, emotions and a history of my own troubles within." If we could walk in another person's shoes and see their life, we would understand them better. I want to be a better person, and I want to forgive all those who have hurt me too. It is over and in the past. We are all new beings in each moment, and we are now free.

I wish to say to all my friends and family who have touched my life, "I love you and thank you for all we have learned. My life would not be the same without you in it. I feel all of you deeply in my heart and soul. When it is my time to leave this world and go to through the next doorway, think of me with good thoughts. I am a father, friend or lover and hope I have touched your life in some way.

It is okay to remember the good and the bad as life is full of a variety of experiences. I have lived a very full life with no regrets, and I did it my way. But it is not easy being me. The day will come when I am on the other side through that door into the next realm of life. Know I am well, happy and will see you again. When we see each other we will hug, kiss and enjoy each other's company once more. I know I will see you; it is a promise. Today I am still here now, but someday that will not be for each of us. I love you all so much."

11-11-11

The day is here, and the change is going to start today. It is a
wonderful day, and it is my birthday. I have been ready for this
day to arrive for 10 years, and was told by my guides that this is
when all would truly unfold for me. I am ready to understand
the deep meanings of life. My past is all fulfilled, and I am not
left wanting. I am all excited and feeling really good, thinking
that I might just pass into the light tonight or that it might
happen when I am asleep.

I am living in San Marcos, California with another spiritual
being named "Sirianna". That is her spiritual name. She is a
wonderful woman and we are connected. She has decided to
take me to see the movie "Cloud Atlas" for my birthday.

11-21-11

It has been 10 days since my birthday, and I am feeling very light headed most of the time. This new energy change has me out of balance. I even fell down today off a ladder and hurt my arm. It is not broken, but is swollen and blue. Sirianna is affected too. She is having a hard time walking. Her leg just gives out and she falls down. We are now looking at each other and wondering what is happening to us. I said it may be because we are really connected.

She has had many afflictions over the years, and I have been a caregiver for her. She has had endometriosis and had her ovaries removed. She has been on hormones and she gets moody now. The doctors say she has fibromyalgia and will be in pain the rest of her life. I really want to help and be there for her. I am a healer and work with her daily. Her pain goes away when I touch her, and when I stop it comes right back. It is frustrating to give help when she does not recover.

12-25-11

It is now Christmas day, and I am still feeling out of balance. Sirianna has been getting worse. She is now in a wheelchair or using a cane. Her sons are home, and she is excited to see them. I am still here and wondering about my future. I really want to help Sirianna. Maybe the change I am feeling is to be giving and to help others.

I have decided to ask Sirianna to marry me and see if she feels the same about me. I asked hers sons and her father if it was okay if I asked her to marry me. They said, "Yes, she would like that." So wanting it to be special and a moment to remember, we went to The Mission Inn in Riverside, California. It is the place where presidents of the United States stay when they visit that area of the country. It is wonderful during that time of year. Millions of lights and the Christmas spirit are everywhere. Sirianna and her sons were there, and she was in her wheelchair. I asked her to stand next to the tree so I could take a picture. I knelt in front of the big Christmas tree in the main room and asked her to marry me. She said, "Yes." It was a wonderful evening.

12-27-11

I am lying down in my room and feeling tired. I am on my back just thinking, hearing a sound coming from my breathing. It sounds a little like "Rice Crispies". It is very odd and pretty loud. I ask Sirianna to come into the room and listen to it. She says that is not good. We should go to the emergency room right now. I said, "I feel fine." She said, "No, we are going right now."

We went to the ER, and they ran some tests on my body. The doctors said the tests showed that my heart was pumping fluid into my lungs, and that was the sound I was hearing. They needed to run more tests, so they admitted me into the hospital. A small surgery had to be done to check my heart, so I said okay and had the surgery the next day.

The findings from the doctors were not good. They said of three main arteries in my heart, two of them were fully blocked. The other one was only at 12% of flowing correctly; I should have had a heart attack, it was so low. They said I could die at any moment, and there would not be much they could do. The best thing for me would be to have a triple heart bypass and put new arteries in my heart. I said I understood and set a date to have the surgery done. It took one month to schedule it, and it was done on January 26, 2012.

I Am Ready

I was ready to leave this world. This was what I thought my guide must have been talking about with a total change, remembering them saying my heart would stop. The surgery took two hours, and the stay in the hospital was five days. The doctors had me on many medications and even morphine. One of the things that does happen when you have this kind of surgery is they stop the heart from beating to replace the arteries.

The surgery went very well, and they said I was in great health. I should recover in two months. They said there could be a few things I needed to watch for now: I must check my blood pressure and watch what I eat. I was also told to walk every day. I knew I could manage that.

Sirianna

Sirianna was not ready to be a caregiver for me. She had troubles of her own as her health was not good and she needed more medications to help with her pain. When I came home to recover, the connection we had ended. We did try to connect one time a month after my surgery, but it never happened. We began to live in separate lives and worlds. The love we thought we shared ended too. She became very paranoid and started hearing things. The drugs were taking their toll on her mind. We never touched or even kissed from that time on.

How could I be so wrong about what I thought would happen in my future. It looked like Sirianna and I were not meant to be together, and getting married was never going to happen. My world had been totally turned upside down, yet still I wanted to help her so I stayed close. I would get the things she needed and make sure she was okay. She almost died three times that year. If I had not been there, she would surely have died. In the end, she did not even go out of the house, keeping the doors locked and windows closed. She did not want to be around people, and ultimately asked me to leave. Neither one of us were happy anymore.

The loss of what could have been is still painful to me.

Love is not an easy thing to just give up and to move on with our lives.

The drugs affected both Sirianna and me so much our lives were now in conflict. She was getting depressed and I was getting paranoid. So intense was my feeling that I started to put items in one spot checking to see if moved and started to hallucinate, seeing things that did not seem real. This went on for weeks, as I was walking around and doing stuff, but everything was still as if I were dead. I wanted more contact with everyone and really needed to feel a connection. Sirianna and I had no connection anymore. My family did not visit or see me, and I was feeling alone and emotional.

I went for a walk to my bank and withdrew all my money thinking maybe I should just keep walking and not look back. I walked for hours and was so exhausted. I did not bring any water with me, and I started to panic. I sat down and thought I could not move one more step. I could hardly breathe, and my heart was pounding. A passing person stopped and looked at me asking if I needed help. I said, "Yes." The ambulance took me back to the hospital. They said I had a panic attack. Here I was with all my money and no water. Sirianna came to the hospital and could not believe I was so stressed. She asked me, "What were you thinking?" I could not answer her and knew our lives had been really changed.

Weeks later, she tried to pull me out and get happy again. She took me to a bar to have a drink. I think she needed it more than me. We were no longer having any fun or doing anything we enjoyed. I had only one drink and I start to hallucinate again, seeing women who were really sexy. I think the drink was making me horny and wanted to connect again with Sirianna. We went home but she did not want me touching her. My body was messed up, and I did not sleep at all that night. Things only got worse, and I fell into a depression, feeling no love in this world. Why did I survive and not die in the hospital? What kind of a change was this? None of it made any sense and I even started to think death was an option. I was being saved for what? Only time would tell me. I must endure this experience. There was more to come, so much more, and things were going to get even worse. This experience was not over and my life was to be tested, yet again. She asked me to leave and not come back or have any contact with her. I left and still feel the loss of what I thought could have been. But it was not to be. My world was now going to change and so was I inside. The awakening of the my spirit and my being.

The Truth of Change

The ugly truth of real change had begun in my life. I have found that you have to get rid of the old and take on the new energy within. Not only did I lose my love and my home, I next lost my job, because I was having a hard time remembering what to do at work. The surgery had many side effects that I was not told about. Memory loss was one of those.

The other side effects of a triple heart bypass were high blood pressure, diabetes if not watched, depression, stress, loss of hearing and staying balanced when walking. Anxiety was setting in, and I had the loss of strength in my muscles, blurred vision and all the side effects of the medications. I was now taking many medications the doctors said I needed to keep my body going properly. I also had a chemical imbalance going on in my brain. The changes within my body were as if I were being rewired to a new way of thinking.

Life is so different when you have to change this much inside and out. It is a real eye-opening experience to find out who your real friends are and who are those that said they were.

The Drugs

The drugs the doctors want you to take after surgery are not really good for you. They are meant to control the body when it should be done naturally. The surgery itself is not natural and is brutal when you really think about. I now have over 10 scars on my body. They took arteries from one leg and put them in my heart. In case of an emergency or complications during surgery, they have to poke three holes just above the belly button. Then there is the main cut down the middle of my chest called a zipper. Strange, but it was like the Aztec ritual of taking the heart out. They give you morphine to ease the pain and that causes a few very vivid dreams. Here is one of them.

I was in a large cave or room. It reminded me of the Carlsbad Caverns in New Mexico. There were people with me, and we were walking from one side of the cave to the other. We could see a large opening at the other end. We had many items with us as we headed to the other side where there was another large room or cave. There were groups of children and adults who needed supplies to help them. It was a long hard journey.

Half way through the room, a group or a gang stopped us. They wanted the items we had. They jumped us with weapons like clubs and knives. I was stabbed four or five times and left for dead. My friends near me were hurt too but not as badly. We had to go back to the start again and get new supplies. We all were crying and wonder how this could have happened.

Back at home we received more help and put together a new set of supplies to take to the other side. We had a goal of helping the others and we were willing to suffer again if needed. The supplies were really needed, and we were determined to get them there. We set out again to help. Half way there, we encountered an even larger group that stopped us. They stood right in front of us, and this time they were crying. Many were saying they were sorry for what had happened to us on our last trip. They understood we were trying to help others, and that we were helpers of all. They gave us back what was stolen and much more too.

All of us were now crying. Love was filling the cave with joy. Our hearts were full of thankfulness. Many of them said they had hoped we would come back, and they wanted us know they understood that sharing love is good and is strong within us all. Only a few can stop the good of others for a moment; good will survive. We arrived in the other room with all the supplies where there was a humble poor village. It was an emotional encounter, and we all felt the love and joy filling our bodies.

The morphine was making me dream strange dreams, so I asked the doctors to stop giving it to me. They said okay and asked how my pain was. I said I did not feel any pain, but my mind was confused and felt like I was already dead. I had the feeling of being dead, yet the world around me was so real. The nurses kept waking me up every two hours to do tests, and I was not getting any deep sleep. I snapped at one of the nurses at 3:00 am. and yelled at her. "Could the test wait just a few more hours until morning?" I needed rest, and was so upset and tired. I was lying there and started to feel bad inside. She was just a nurse doing her job and following what the doctors wanted. I could not sleep and it bothered me. So I buzzed the nurse station and asked the nurse I yelled at to come back in. I said I was sorry and understood what she was trying to do. She said it was okay and not to worry about it. The next day she came in and gave me a big red stuffed heart pillow. She said it was to say thank you. All the nurses at the station signed it. It is good to know that people care about other people and their feelings. I was in the hospital only five days and was released. Then went home with more drugs and the feeling this was not over.

A New Life

My change of life is in full swing. I lost my job, lost my home and lost my fiancée too. I was making so much money earlier, and yet I had no real savings. My family could not help, and most of my friends wanted to help but were not able to. So I started to live in my car. I had no cell phone. I never thought this could happen to me. The state of California was not really much help either. All the shelters were full, and there are many homeless people out there. I was safe and had found a good place to park my car each night. I applied for assistance and received food stamps. They gave me $180 a month for food. That is $6 a day and only just enough to live on and survive. My medical care also was now from the state of California.

I was going to sleep at 10:30 and waking up at sunrise. I have been very lucky that a few friends have helped me with gas and a few dollars to do laundry. I want to thank all those who have really helped me survive. It was so hard to get some of the things that are needed to just live and survive. There is a fitness club in San Marcos where I worked out daily. It has a nice shower and place for me to change clothes.

My only connection to the world is the Internet. There is a Starbucks close by and they have free Wi-Fi available. It is really strange to realize you are a homeless person. Everyone who knows me would never think of me in that way.

A New Point of View

Walking is what I do every day. Two to five miles is really good for my heart, and it is enjoyable to do, seeing all the beauty the world has to offer and watching people interact. Sunsets and the early sunrise are my favorites. My preferred places to walk are within 10 miles. The beach in Carlsbad, California has a nice boardwalk, and everyone loves walking there. Walking next to the ocean gives me many great feelings. I get to connect with the earth walking in the sand and ocean. It is calm and peaceful. I try to walk a different way each day and observe how friendly or not people are during their day. Most of them are in their own worlds, and some even never make eye contact. It is nice, though, when people pass and smile or say hello. They are sharing the world around them.

I do see many in a survival mode too. There are those who are homeless and begging for money. Some are looking for food or even a place of shelter from the elements. There are thousands of them now all across the United States of America. I used to ask myself: "What happened to them?" Each has a different story, and I can see the pain in their eyes. Some look as if they were beaten, and their minds are going through the motions of existence. When people look at them, they look the other way or pretend they do not exist. They are lost souls in a sea of constant struggle. What happened to their jobs or their family? Did they have a life or shelter before? Their minds seem to suffer from the loss of what they had before. The people I see who are homeless are from many different places, and every day they feel the abuse from others around them. No one seems to care what happens to them. Every day they keep surviving somehow, some who were in an accident or are handicapped or mentally ill. They keep wanting each day to connect to someone. Many use signs or stop people at stores to see if they have change to spare. Most people feel afraid of them or walk the other way. But, they just want to survive.

I have found the best way to connect with them, I walk right up to them and say hi, letting them know I do not have any money either. I ask them how things have been going for them. Just a simple conversation with another person and listening to them is a great help. Many have not talked with another person about anything in a long time. The only people they usually talk to are other homeless. They may not have had any kindness like a hug in months or even years. All want a little hope that things might get better. Everyone in this world should have three things: food, shelter and the feeling they are loved. I do hope they receive those basic things each day and their hearts are healed inside. Loving themselves is the best start to getting the feeling of hope.

Body and Mind

My body and mind are starting to fail me. As we get older, it slowly gets harder to do what we did in the past. I wonder how long my body will last. I used to run and play tennis every day. Those days may never happen again. My memories are fading too. It is hard to remember the little things each day. People tell me something, and the next day I cannot remember what they said. It is a little scary when even 10 or 15 minutes after a conversation I may not recall it. Names of people are blurry or I cannot think of them. My eyes seem to still see well, and yet I do need glasses for some things. I did have cataract surgery on both eyes in my 40s. My hearing is now at about 50% and slowly getting worse. Funny how life goes on, and I am becoming deaf, blind and stupid.

The future is so unknown for me now. I always had a plan and thought of what my next project should be: where I should be, or with whom I am to be. I knew what my path was and what direction I should choose. Now for the first time, I am letting the universe chose. I am letting each day unfold in front of me truly living moment to moment. There is so much freedom in that, and yet fear of the unknown creeps into my thoughts.

When alone I am pondering why am I here. Where should I be? Life and death are becoming a grey area in my soul's existence. It feels like a dream being played out in front of me as each moment passes by. Where am I really? Did I die? Are these just memories? If so why? These are some of the thoughts that float through my mind when I am alone.

Maybe it is the lack of sleep I get each night, waking up every two hours to pee. My prostate is enlarged and cannot hold water very long now. I cannot remember the last time I got a full night's sleep of eight hours. I even took a few sleeping pills once, but that made me feel odd in the morning. I am not taking any medications now. Even aspirin affects me, and I bleed. Right now my body is clean of all medications.

I am still walking two to five miles a day and working out for two hours every day at the gym. I am working on my health and upper body, and getting some strength in my arms. At least I am not falling down anymore. My balance is getting better with each day. I am trying to make this mind and body last until the universe decides to take me. A sadness and depression comes over me, though when I think of my future. My life is at a crossroads. Life and death are blurred inside me. I am confused and feeling alone.

When I feel like this, I often write. Last time I felt this way, I wrote this down and prayed.

My Heart
Today it beats like a drum
Still wants to stop its Harmony

It has failed

No one sees me

I have so much love to share

Give inside

In my soul

And Darkness it hides

Pain washes over me

Death wants a partner

I want to live

Rejoice in love shared

My cries go across the universe

In hopes it cared

Silence is all

No word

My thoughts wander

Hopes that this will all end

Breathing has almost stopped

The lack of communication

It leaves me in a hole of desperation

I try to crawl to the surface

My Soul needs a purpose

Creator of all that exists

Please

Give me a sign and hope

My Heart

Still Beats

I wrote this book in my book and was written because of how I was feeling as these new changes came over me. This poem was my sign and a gift to me. My focus and purpose were revealed.

Who is Dane Whitecloud Now?

I am a soft spoken, humble man who loves nature and connecting with good friends. The feelings of caring fill me deep inside each day. I am a gentle man in every sense of the word. My world is about helping others and respecting all, wanting everyone to be the best they can be in life. Deep inside I have feeling of connection to all people.

My few possessions are meaningless. The only thing I really desire is love and caring. I seek the love that is given freely and unconditionally in a meaningful connection of one person to another in a simple natural way. Because we both have learned that love is precious. Love is in us all, but when it is shared it grows and takes over your being in a beautiful way. My heart is so full of love and the need to share it. I am hoping someone will accept it freely and want it. It is yours to enjoy and feel if you want it.

It has taken a few lifetimes to be who I am today. In this life of 60 years, many thousands of people have touched me in many ways. Some of them for only a few moments and others have been lifelong friends. There are those who are still living and those who have passed on through the door of life. I wish to express my thanks for all you have done for me. You have enlightened me and changed my thoughts on so many levels of understanding. Each of us has something to share with others in our life and our experiences.

I know I have affected others too. Some people know what I have done and others do not. We are all so connected and part of the fabric of being human. It is all the good and the bad of life. It has an effect on us spiritually and on our understanding. Who we are inside feels all of the changes.

To all the beautiful beings of light that have cared for me in so many ways, I thank you for the love you have shown me. The feeling of joy touches me daily. You have put your arms around me during all of my ups and downs. My guides have been there every step with me. You have given me guidance and direction, hope without judgment. Every moment of my life you have been there.

When thinking of this world and the other worlds beyond in lightness or darkness, I am also touched. You who I have met in the mansion worlds have helped me become the being I am today. Thank you so much; I want to continue being touched by what you do for me.

To the creator of all that exists I want to say "Wow!!!" What an experience you have given me. All I have is because you wished it. The gift of life and sharing in the expansion of caring is beyond words. The journey is so beautiful and a wonder to be a part of. So many happy feelings fill my heart each day of my life. I was created to experience this and so much more, and I will continue as a being with thought. Thank you from the depth of my heart.

A Moment of Harmony

Slow your mind down for a moment. Take three deep breaths, and walk outside in the garden of the world around you. Sit down and take a good look. I want you to take three more deep breaths and slow your mind down one more time.

You may see people, trees or whatever may be around you. See the beauty in all of them. As you look, lower your eyes to the ground. See what is at your feet. You may see a planter or the base of a tree. It could be just the grass. Whatever you see, it is right in front of you. Did you realize there is a whole world at your feet? It is a world of peace and harmony. You look at the plants that are growing in this moment. There is a connection, and they are sharing this moment with you. Feel the calmness within them. They take in energy from the sun and the wind moves them softly. If you look even closer, you will see the insects that move and crawl around. They are living in harmony and peace with nature.

As you keep looking deeper, you may even see drops of water feeding all that lives. What a peaceful existence; it is so beautiful. It does not matter where you are on planet earth. There is this calm world at your feet. It is happening all over the world at this very moment. The very large and the very small have so much beauty and harmony. We are a part of it every day of our lives. Every cell that lives in existence feels that moment of life. They too are one with us, and I am thankful they are here. It makes me calm and in harmony.

Tonight

I look up at the stars in the sky as the clouds pass over head. The soft white clouds call out my name inside of me. My name is Whitecloud, and the reason I was given that name passes over my head each day. I am not of this planet, and I am not in the stars at this moment. I am right in between them floating in observation in the clouds. Across the sky they move on the wind, as the planet moves underneath them with amazing speed. I feel so much a part of the dance of the planets and nature. As I look deep into the cosmos, I see the number of stars that are glowing back at me. Following the dance and flowing across in front of me, they seem to blink just for me. Peaceful and calmly moving, they are doing what they do, and the movement is constant every moment of their existence. It is so beautiful, and I am a part of it all. I think to myself: Thank You. It is such a gift to be where I am and seeing this wonderful sight. It happens every day and every night for you and me. It touches my soul.

Being Alone

I'm not sure if you can do it, but I want everyone in this world to think for a moment. You can be sitting anywhere on the planet. This is what you have to picture in your mind. You do not have a job, a home, a family or friends. You know no one and no one knows you. Your existence has no meaning to anyone around you. Do you feel the separation? Do you feel sadness or at peace? The human experience is one of interactions. We are social, and our culture is one of contact. Just a smile or a hello can make us feel connected to our world. We do so many things in life to make us feel like we are connected to others. Are we truly connected? Are we feeling the deep inner connection?

Most of us go through life never understanding the deeper connections of life. If we were to stop and make a real connection as a being of light, it would change the world. When you reach out from deep within yourself and touch another deep within, it is magical. It says to the world: thank you for being alive in this moment of experience; thank you for being with me in mind, body and spirit. A smile of caring and love fill you as you look into their eyes. You see them, and they see you. It is a beautiful thing to share a moment of energy passing between souls. It can fill your heart, and your hearts beat as one.

Life on this world is about those moments of connection. I hope every day of my life and yours you will have a few of them. In this moment I thank you and the universe for my experience. It fills me with joy and love. We're all one and I'm glad. To all my connections I have had in this world, I say, "Thank you!"

The reason you're reading about my life and what happened to me in the last few years is it took a triple heart bypass and the loss of all I held dear to me to awaken. You don't have to suffer to become aware and have your eyes opened. If I can touch just one of you today, my pain will be worth it all. Share your experiences with others. Change lives. And love unconditionally.

Printed in the United States
By Bookmasters